5 VIEWS ON THE FUTURE OF YOUTH MINISTRY
Perspectives on What Could or Should Be

Mark Oestreicher, General Editor
Contributors:
Chris Curtis
Kenda Creasy Dean
Mark DeVries
Tommy Nixon
Virginia Ward

5 VIEWS ON THE FUTURE OF YOUTH MINISTRY

Publisher: Mark Oestreicher
Managing Editor: Sarah Hauge
Cover Design and Layout: Marilee Pankratz
Creative Director: Nostradamus

ISBN-13: 978-1-942145-62-2

The Youth Cartel, LLC
www.theyouthcartel.com
Email: info@theyouthcartel.com

Born in San Diego.
Printed in the U.S.A.

CONTENTS

INTRODUCTION

MARK OESTREICHER

Way back in the early aughts (that's the early 2000s, to be clear), I was given something of a platform for prognosticating to the youth ministry tribe. I was the president of an influential youth ministry training organization called Youth Specialties, and as part of that role, I got to give the closing general session talk at the National Youth Workers Convention for a bunch of years in a row, in three cities each fall. This meant I was giving a "sending out charge" to something like 10,000 to 15,000 youth workers each year (for the record: my "platform" is comparatively tiny these days, and I love it).

I chose to be a provocateur.

Maybe I was called to that role. Maybe? No question, though, some part of this was my choice, born more out of ego than Holy Spirit-leading. That acknowledged, I said (and wrote) some things that weren't completely inaccurate about our need for significant change in our thinking and practice of youth ministry. But when I look back on that body of work (that's a generous term—maybe I should just call it my "central themes"?), 99% of it was focused on what we needed to *stop doing*. Without going into all the details, the condensed version of my message was, "Don't you see? We're doing it wrong!"

I'd already been friends with Kurt Johnston for years at that point. Kurt was, at that time, the junior high pastor at a massive church in Southern California, not too far from where I live, and we shared a passion for ministry to young teens. Kurt and I have a friendship that doesn't always make sense in a world where most of us only develop meaningful relationships with people we agree with, because Kurt and I disagree on many things, including many theological points. But the friendship is real, and we both enjoy the tension.

As I was getting louder and more focused in my "We're doing it wrong!" message, Kurt kept gently pushing back with suggestions that

God was still at work, that great things were still happening in pretty much every youth ministry, and that (to use his constant words) "the sky is not falling."

All these years later, Kurt and I have likely both moved closer to the middle point between our previously polarized perspectives. I mean, he wasn't totally wrong back then, but neither was I (his character was better, though). There's been great movement in the collective thinking of youth workers over the last two decades, beginning to address many of the things I (and others) thought were broken or outdated. But God is still working, and Jesus is still pursuing every teenager—before, during, and after they're involved in our ministries. And so many wonderful things are happening in thousands of youth ministries you've never heard of, and never will.

Why Youth Workers Like Thinking About the Future

Whatever your age, I think youth workers *tend to* be some of the most future-oriented people in church leadership. It's not that senior pastors or children's workers or worship leaders don't think about the future (shoot, just look at all the books about change and the future written for senior clergy), but rather that youth workers who *aren't* future-oriented often get weeded out over time.

We're generally hopeful people. Not that you're a hope-monster at every moment, of course. But because youth ministry is just SO FREAKING HARD, people don't last long if they don't have a sense, a commitment, that God continues to author a story even if we can't see it. When my seventh grade guys small group has a particularly unproductive meeting (which, if I'm honest, is roughly 50% of them, maybe more), I can only find the grit to return the next week because I hope for what I do not yet have, and wait for it patiently (that's roughly Romans 8:25, if it sounds familiar).

Youth ministry has less accurate feedback loops than pretty much any other ministry in the church. Little kids are either stoked to be there and paying attention or they're not. Adults vote with their feet and provide positive and negative feedback. But my most unruly seventh grade guy—the one who regularly wears me down to a nub—pulled me aside to pray for me a couple weeks ago when he knew I was dealing with a hard issue. What do I do with that (other than allow it to fuel my hope)?

We're generally change-oriented. I recently had a little "a-ha" about this reality. Animals, as I'm sure you know, tend to move into fight, flight, or freeze when a potential threat comes into their field of senses. But the healthy option, which you might *not* have heard of—the fourth option—is to orient. For an animal, this means they do *not* fight, freeze, or run away. Instead, they adjust. You *cannot* work with teenagers for long if you don't learn how to orient. In conversations, in teaching, in small group leadership, even in programming. We youth workers are trained, by our audience, to orient. This means that we naturally and progressively learn to be change-oriented, which often results in reflecting about the future.

We work with people leaning toward the future. Children (mostly) live in the present. Adults are all over the place, but the older they get, the less they tend to live for the future (and many live for the past). But those amazing teenagers: They're obsessed with the future. They might be pumped about it or terrified about it, but "next" is a constant thought.

The Future of Youth Ministry: Then and Now

In 2010 (just after the aughts!), after I'd moved on from Youth Specialties, I was asked to lead a seminar at the National Youth Workers Convention on The Future of Youth Ministry. To prepare for this, I sent an email to a dozen national youth ministry thinkers and asked them to give me a few sentences about how they saw the future. One of those responders was Dr. Kenda Dean of Princeton Theological Seminary, whom I consider to be our MIBIYMT (that's our Most Important Brain in Youth Ministry Today). The two paragraphs she sent me—about the need for us to "re-weirdify Christianity"—took my breath away, and all these years later, were the nexus for this book.

But I thought it might be interesting to go back to some of those comments from 2010 and invite a few people to update their words. I'd like to share four of those here. I'm wondering if you'll see the same tonal shift I see. In some ways, this parallels the personal shift I've gone through, which I alluded to in the opening paragraphs, a shift from "not that" to "this," from "what we're doing wrong" to "what positive steps we need to take."

Dr. Kara Powell of Fuller Theological Seminary (and the Fuller Youth Institute) wrote, in 2010:
> *I think the future of youth ministry is one in which the age-segregation that has dominated the church ends and we move toward the type of intergenerational community and integration God intends. We're seeing in our research how important intergenerational community and relationships are to Sticky Faith.*

Kara's new statement:
> *The future of youth ministry hinges on the church focusing on what matters most. It's about adults staying intimately connected to Jesus, and helping this wonderfully diverse generation grasp that Jesus best satisfies their hunger for identity, belonging, and purpose.*

Kurt Johnston of Saddleback Church in Orange County, California, wrote words in 2010 that I've already referenced:
> *Youth ministry is too nuanced…too fluid…to predict its future with any level of certainty. I do not believe the youth ministry sky is falling and look forward to a bright future, in whatever shape it takes.*

Now he writes:
> *The lessons learned from 2020 combined with the reality that youth ministry is an ever-evolving living organism makes me more hesitant than ever before to try to predict what its future will look like. One prediction I feel somewhat comfortable making is that I think youth ministries will begin to draw stronger theological lines in the sand, identify their distinctives more clearly, and be bolder in the ways they communicate their message to teenagers.*

Greg Stier of Dare 2 Share Ministries was super concise in 2010:
> *In the future, the church will be forced to marginalize or centralize youth ministry…no in-between.*

Today he sure sounds more hopeful to me:
> *The future of youth ministry is not more and better programs, it's clearer and more focused mission. A decade from now teenagers*

won't be satisfied with just "going to youth group" but will whole-heartedly embrace going on mission for Christ with their youth group. Youth leaders that continue down the road of typical youth group done in the typical way will see diminishing results. Those who champion a Gospel advancing, disciple-multiplying, teen-activating approach will see their youth groups not just survive, but thrive. The future of youth ministry depends on whether or not youth leaders embrace this radical new paradigm in youth ministry (that's actually 2,000 years old).

And finally, **Dr. Steven Argue**, who is now with Kara at Fuller Theological Seminary, but was doing a variety of consulting and teaching in Michigan back in 2010, wrote some decidedly strong and punchy words:

Hey church, adolescents are NOT leaving you. You are perpetually leaving them. Stop using statistical bullshit to project blame. Repent. Unless you're willing to let adolescents mess with your own life, you have no business messing with their lives. Most churches are not worthy of youth pastors. Youth pastors, stop giving yourself to organizations that use you to better "market" their church to families; that expect you to "produce" programs; and that exploit you because they know it's hard to leave the kids you love. Walk away. Don't take the job, because if you do, you're wrecking it for all of us. Raise the bar. Boycott churches unworthy of youth pastors. Amen.

These days, Steve is feeling more poetic, apparently, as he sent me these gorgeous words that read like a sonnet:

I still worry about what I wrote ten years ago because I lament seeing amazing youth leaders who truly care about young people get boxed in by churches and organizations that lack imagination.

*Maybe another way to say it is that, perhaps,
the best youth ministry doesn't happen in the spotlight of "wow,"
the best youth leaders have few social media followers,
the best youth ministries may not even look like "youth ministry."
I have grown to find these to be more interesting, more holy.*

Youth ministries must not be tempted to use teenagers to justify their existence,

instead, they must keep seeking to understand teenagers,
always adjusting to see and hear them more clearly,
supporting young people where they say they need youth ministry the
most.

Here are the decentered, messy, sacred spaces
where young people travel
where Jesus is
and where youth ministry must faithfully go.

A Bit of Orientation

As much as I'd like to leave it there, with Steve's beautiful (and hopeful) final verse, you would benefit, I believe, from a bit of framing for what you're about to read.

Choosing the five contributors for this book was a hefty challenge. I knew we needed Kenda to expand her thoughts about "re-weirdifying" Christianity. And I'd heard Mark DeVries speak a few times about his views about the future, and knew we wanted him on this project. Then I created a big ol' list of possibilities—some with themes, some without—and started asking people. And the mix of five we ended up with is, I have to acknowledge, pretty amazing.

In our previous three multi-views books (*4 Views on Pastoring LGBTQ Teenagers*, *4 Views on Talking to Teenagers About Sex*, and *5 Views on Youth Ministry Short-Term Missions*), we chose contributors who covered a spectrum of thought, but were also in the trenches actively doing youth ministry and living out the ideas they wrote about. Then we had each of them write a response to one of the other chapters, pairing them with contributors who had very different perspectives from their own.

But for this book, our contributors are less day-to-day youth workers and more thought leaders. So, instead of having them respond to each other's chapters, I chose to go a different route: We asked each chapter writer to connect us with a (younger) in-the-trenches youth worker who was already living into the future their chapter proposed. This adds some rich story to this collection, as well as a clear sense that *this is possible.*

I hope you find this book challenging, and I trust it will stir your imagination. More than provoking you, I pray it will encourage you. And heck, let's lean into the bulk of the book with Steve Argue's final words after all:

Here are the decentered, messy, sacred spaces
where young people travel
where Jesus is
and where youth ministry must faithfully go.

—Marko

VIEW 1:
STRANGER THINGS:
EMBRACING THE ODDNESS
OF JESUS IN YOUTH
MINISTRY

BY KENDA CREASY DEAN

None of us can ever express the exact measure of [our] needs or thoughts or sorrows. Human speech is like a cracked kettle on which we tap crude rhythms for bears to dance to—while we long to make music that will melt the stars.

—Gustave Flaubert, *Madame Bovary*

In May 2020—a shipwreck of a year, if ever there was one—*Fast Company* asked business leaders how COVID-19 was changing their industries. Colleen DeCourcy, copresident and chief creative officer of the world's largest independent advertising firm, was succinct: "I think this could be the death of bullshit."[1] Alluding to advertising norms that privilege style over substance, words over action, self-interest over service, proclamation over perspiration, DeCourcy wondered aloud about the industry's self-deception: "What did [our work] *do*? What did it do for the brand? What did it do for *people*?"

She meant advertising. Of course.

I winced. It was a little close. What *does* our work do? What does youth ministry do for faith? What does it do for young people? How much have *we* been deceiving ourselves—or the young people we love?

Time to Stop Kidding Ourselves

Rewind to Valentine's Day 2018. A tragic school shooting at Marjory Stoneman Douglas High School in Parkland, Florida, left seventeen people dead, a nation reeling, and high school students enraged and galvanized with purpose. In her speech at a gun control rally in Fort Lauderdale three days later, seventeen-year-old Emma Gonzalez famously "called B.S.":

> The people in government who were voted into power are lying to us. And us kids seem to be the only ones who notice… They say tougher gun laws do not decrease gun violence—*we call B.S.* They say a good guy with a gun stops a bad guy with a gun—*we call B.S.* They say guns are just tools like knives and are as dangerous as cars—*we call B.S.* They say no laws could have prevented the hundreds of senseless tragedies that have occurred—*we call B.S.* That us kids don't know what we're talking about, that we're too young to understand how the government works—*we call B.S.*[2]

I happened to speak at a youth ministry event in Parkland the weekend following the shootings. I was sure the event would be cancelled; okay, I desperately hoped it would be cancelled. Surely the best response to such world-shattering pain would be silence. But then Julie, the organizer, called to let me know they had added a vigil to the weekend's schedule. Yes, the event was surely happening. "If faith is ever going to matter to people here," she said, "it needs to matter *now*." So, I packed.

In fact, this event had been planned in part by one of Parkland's victims, sixteen-year-old Carmen Schentrup, president of the diocesan youth group, who was gunned down in her A.P. psychology class.[3] The teachers, youth leaders, and parents attending the diocesan event moved slowly, weighed down by collective exhaustion. Many had been planning—and all had been attending—funerals all week. Everyone had stories of trauma that they recounted in acute detail, as though telling them one more time could blunt the anguish. Most local teens, I was told, were holed up in various family rooms that weekend, making furious plans to descend on the state capitol on Wednesday. It was a trip destined to disappoint; three days later, teenagers would hear one lawmaker after another recite, with eerie precision, the very excuses Gonzalez enumerated in her speech.[4]

14

At the end of the youth ministry event, the local bishop offered closing remarks. He emphasized how proud he was of Parkland's young people—proud of the way they had mobilized their grief, leveraged the media, and were feverishly working to transform tragedy into action. But, he said, he was worried. Would these efforts prove to be "big enough," he wondered, to hold young people in this tragic moment? Did the institutions that these teenagers were trusting to dismantle evil have the courage to confront it—or would this same evil ultimately derail their earnest efforts, exhaust their good intentions, and quash their passionate spirits? "And evil *will* come," the bishop warned. "Evil *always* comes when God is on the move." Inevitably, he noted, the teens would tire. Inevitably, the unsated news cycle would move on. Inevitably, time would dim their grief and good intentions— graduation, college, jobs, life would all press Parkland's teens to put this awful moment behind them. As urgent as their message was, as convicted as they were, as courageous as they had become, the movement could easily wither, the bishop warned us. Activism, the democratic process, the sheer chutzpah of teenagers—do these have the fortitude to withstand evil? He didn't think so.

So then…what?

Re-Weirdifying Christianity

The question the bishop left hanging in the air was whether the church offered anything better. What the young people of Parkland sought— what we all seek, as Flaubert observed—is music so fierce that it melts the stars—yet on most days those of us in ministry bang out our small tunes on cracked kettles and dance like bears.[5] Instead of offering young people a story that looks death squarely in the eye and turns devastation on its head with resurrection and hope, we are prone to offering them a story that is less weird, less risky. The story we often offer young people is about a God who won't keep them up at night—a decaffeinated Christianity—rather than a God who asks for a way of life that could get them crucified. The truth is, like the American church generally, most of us in youth ministry are excellent at ministry that helps young people fit into, and take part in, "the American way": they become skilled consumers and self-actualized individualists, albeit with a religious twist. Which is to say, as Christian discipleship, it is "bullshit."

If twenty-first century youth ministry is to matter—if it is to survive as *ministry*—then we need to take stock. Line up people who profess Christ beside people who profess nothing in particular—is Jesus recognizable in us? Compare youth ministry to a bevy of good-for-you extracurricular activities available to young people after school—is there anything that sets us apart? If not, then it is time to "re-weirdify" Christianity, embracing the oddness of Jesus in ways that make Christianity "strange" again for young people and those who love them. As we will see, most of us are guilty of squeezing the weirdness straight out of the gospel until God is a tame puppy in the other room, who comes when called to perform certain tricks for us, but otherwise stays out of our way. In this domesticated gospel, Jesus gives us a friendly thumbs up (no matter what) and the Holy Spirit is a pleasant breeze in April. As theology goes, it feels a lot like a Thomas Kinkade painting that has been in the sun too long.

Youth ministries that invite the oddness of Jesus, on the other hand, foster more Emma Gonzalezes than Emma Woodhouses, more Greta Thunbergs than Richie Cunninghams—young people who are hard to embrace but impossible to ignore. Such ministries consistently deliver exhausting young people who challenge us. Yet these youth ministries cannot exist apart from the church, either. Young people "re-weirdified" by Jesus may be pained by what churches have become; they may even create alternative expressions of Christ's Body in which they more easily see themselves.[6] But their critiques are born out of longing to be Christ's hands and feet in the world in ways that are transparent and true. When young people embrace Jesus's weirdness, they can justly be accused—like disciples before them—of "turning the world upside down" for Christ (Acts 17:6-7, NRSV). Nothing makes most religious organizations feel more at risk. Nothing makes most teenagers feel more alive.

It is an old sin, acculturated Christianity—and it is as dangerous to youth ministry now as it was for Paul and Timothy. The choice for the church in every age is, "Will our identity be shaped by the gospel or by our culture—by God's story or by our cultural story?"[7] We are all prone to fashion the gods we can live with instead of following the God who chose to live with us. Humans consistently create the gods we can stomach—gods who share our tastes and values, biases and ambitions. When "good Christian people" invoke Christ's name while instigating unthinkable evil, we rightly recoil and wonder, "What kind of God would sanction such a thing?" The answer is: The god we have fashioned in our own image, who approves the evils we like best.[8]

Mounting data reveals how cozy youth ministry has become with some of these golden calves. Scan online curriculum for youth groups and you'll find endless lessons that show how being a Christian makes you nicer (you'll make good choices), helps you feel happier (you'll feel blessed and fulfilled), and assists you in navigating a world where God hovers harmlessly in the background. This particular religious outlook, which sociologists have dubbed "moralistic therapeutic deism" (see *Figure 1.1*), might seem Christian-ish at first glance, but scratch the surface and you'll find more Oprah than Yahweh, more Thomas Jefferson than Jesus. Moralistic therapeutic deism may not be wholly objectionable, but it doesn't transform anything, either. In short, moralistic therapeutic deism reveals the fact that we proclaim a bigger story than we practice; we promise teenagers resurrection but deliver them pizza. To borrow the words of Emma Gonzales, the "kids" seem to be the only ones who notice that they're being deceived. Look at young people's declining participation in faith communities. Look at their easy compartmentalization of religious belief. Look at their growing religious disaffiliation. They are calling B.S.

Losing Our Oddness:
The Rise of Moralistic Therapeutic Deism

For many of us, this is all a tiresome review. It has now been more than a decade since Christian Smith and Melinda Lundquist Denton published their first findings from the decade-long National Study of Youth and Religion—including the much-discussed view that most North American teenagers (like most North Americans) adhere to a bland, generic religiosity that researchers called moralistic therapeutic deism. Moralistic therapeutic deism is a superficial do-good, feel-good spirituality in which a generic God exists but is mostly unnecessary. Instead of humans responding to God, moralistic therapeutic deism expects God to respond to humans. In moralistic therapeutic deism, we are not made for God; God is made for us.

1	A GOD EXISTS WHO CREATED AND ORDERED THE WORLD, AND WATCHES OVER HUMAN LIFE ON EARTH.
2	GOD WANTS PEOPLE TO BE GOOD, NICE, AND FAIR TO EACH OTHER, AS TAUGHT IN THE BIBLE AND BY MOST WORLD RELIGIONS.
3	THE CENTRAL GOAL OF LIFE IS TO BE HAPPY AND TO FEEL GOOD ABOUT YOURSELF.
4	GOD DOES NOT NEED TO BE INVOLVED IN MY LIFE, EXCEPT WHEN I NEED GOD TO RESOLVE A PROBLEM.
5	GOOD PEOPLE GO TO HEAVEN WHEN THEY DIE.

Figure 1.1, the 5 Tenets of Moralistic Therapeutic Deism[9]

Line up these tenets of moralistic therapeutic deism alongside, say, the Apostles' Creed—just one précis of historic Christian teachings—and the contrasts become evident.[10] But MTD *does* align nicely with values like self-determination, congeniality, consumerism, and therapeutic individualism—all keys to success in middle-class America. In fact, write Smith and Denton,

> It seems to us [that] Moralistic Therapeutic Deism is colonizing many historic religious traditions and, almost without anyone noticing, converting believers from the old faiths to its alternative religious vision of divinely underwritten personal happiness and interpersonal niceness.[11]

No wonder much of the world (and many Americans) confuse being Christian with being an American citizen. Moralistic therapeutic deism, as it turns out, makes for excellent citizens—which is to say, it lets young people be more wholesome than holy, superficially religious without being odd.

Losing Our Moorings for Jesus

The problem, of course, is that the gospel *is* odd, and unless youth ministry embraces the oddness of Jesus, we are very apt to form young people into moralistic therapeutic deists instead of Christians, no matter what their baptism certificates say. I use the word "odd" intentionally. It comes from a Norse word for a triangular piece of land, indicating the "arrow tip" of land that points beyond the two base points. When Vikings brought the word to England, it became a way to describe something without a mate or a peer, which by the fifteenth century meant you were "outstanding" or "illustrious" (i.e., "peerless"). It took another 200 years for the word to mean "peculiar" or "eccentric."[12]

It is precisely Christianity's illustrious peculiarity that North American churches seem to have abandoned. Jesus proclaimed (and embodied) an "upside down kingdom" in which the established ways of the world are turned on their head. Isaiah proclaimed these inversions the marks of the true Messiah (Isaiah 35:5-6). When John the Baptist asks Jesus's followers if Jesus is the one they've been waiting for, Jesus sends back the messianic signature: "Go and tell John what you have seen and heard: the blind receive their sight, the lame walk, the lepers are cleansed, the deaf hear, the dead are raised, the poor have good news brought to them" (Luke 7:22, NRSV).

Who can be silent at such astonishing news? "Mission," wrote Lesslie Newbigin, "begins with an explosion of joy"—but explosions are disruptive, blowing holes in taken-for-granted power structures and habits of polite society.[13] Acculturated Christianity blunts our ability to follow Jesus Christ by rounding the corners of the most challenging parts of the story: The journey to the cross is tamed into a Sunday stroll, Paul's famous image of dying to self is reduced to an inconvenience of time or money. It's true that Jesus's invitation to participate in a love worthy of suffering is the dimension of Christian life most apt to go wrong in human hands. Originally, the word "suffering" meant to be overwhelmed by, or to be vulnerable to, another—to "suffer" love, for instance.[14] Today, of course, we equate "suffering" with unbidden anguish, which changes the calculus. We rightly shun religious practices that sanction abuse or glorify self-mortification. We rightly protest interpretations of Scripture that seem to make suffering a goal in itself. Youth leaders are justifiably on alert for such perverse theologies, since they so easily play into teenagers' tendencies toward excess.[15]

Still, sacrificial, self-giving love is fundamental to following Jesus, and to a holy life that imitates Christ, which is clearly further than interpersonal niceness and personal happiness will go. Typically—

and with the best of intentions—most of us batten down the hatches *against* holiness. In Scripture, holy people are wise but weird; everyone admires them, but no one wants their children to be like them. We want our children to succeed, to be moral, happy people—so we want youth ministry to create "sober virgins," not holy weirdos.[16] For the past fifty years, as churches ramped up their emphasis on young people, our impulse has been to tie down youth ministry's floppy corners on the moorings of cultural fit and professional respectability. To be clear, I've contributed my share to this movement. Yet despite enormous gains made in youth ministry since the 1970s, we have moved to the shallow end of the pool where we risk less and splash more—largely thanks to two culprits: the rise of moralistic therapeutic deism in American churches, and the success of the "youth ministry industry." Here's what I mean:

1. The Culprit of Colonization:
The Rise of Moralistic Therapeutic Deism
Middle-class life in the United States extols the virtues of getting along: be nice, feel happy, nod to a god but don't bow to one. The National Study of Youth and Religion noted the importance of such an outlook for "lubricating" human relationships; flattening distinctions between religious groups is a very useful strategy for creating common ground in a pluralistic culture, even if it is not Scriptural advice. Jesus's consistent strategy, by contrast, was to profoundly value each person in her particularity, loving her in her distinctiveness rather than homogenizing her with others. Compassion and mercy (about which Jesus had much to say) are infinitely more difficult than "getting along" (about which Jesus says nothing).

The NSYR considers the blurred lines between Christian identity and moralistic therapeutic deism as being less about secularization than colonization. "Either Christianity is… degenerating into a pathetic version of itself," write Smith and Denton, or "Christianity is actively being colonized and displaced by a quite different faith."[17] Then they drop this bombshell observation:

> We have come with some confidence to believe that a significant part of Christianity in the United States is actually only tenuously Christian in any sense that is seriously connected to the actual

historical Christian tradition, but has rather substantially morphed into Christianity's misbegotten stepcousin, Christian Moralistic Therapeutic Deism. . . . This has happened in the minds and hearts of many believers and, it also appears, within the structures of at least some Christian organizations and institutions.[18]

In other words, since young people closely mirror the faith of the adults who love them, young people are not moralistic therapeutic deists because they have misunderstood what we have taught them in church. They are moralistic therapeutic deists because *this is what we have taught them* in church.

Young people are the truth-tellers in this scenario. They may think of themselves as Christians, but they find their faith difficult to distinguish from "being a good person." Cassia, age fourteen, is a case in point:

> I do consider myself religious. I'm a Christian, I do believe that there is a higher power, I'm just not exactly....I don't know how to say it...There's a lot of stuff in the Bible that was written there that is kind of weird. I'm not sure how to feel about this. I just believe that everyone should be treated well, forgiven. I'm so bad at explaining my religious feelings. I just want to be a good person, you know, like Jesus' way. I just want to help people.[19]

To be sure, many young people do assume distinctive, even robust, religious identities; in the NSYR one in twelve young people interviewed fell into this "highly devoted" category, and 40% said religion mattered to them.[20] More recent studies define religious devotion differently, and raise different questions.[21] In a 2020 Springtide random sample of 10,000 13- to 25-year-olds, 71% considered themselves at least slightly "religious" but more than half said they didn't trust the religious institutions they were part of. Two in five considered themselves religiously unaffiliated (though one in five of those attended religious services). The same number of young people affiliated with a religious tradition denied being religious people.[22] Young people seem more likely to align with religion than to consider it a force that stirs the soul. It is not the hot lava core of young people's identities, and it is certainly not worth dying over.

Youth are *absolutely* right about this: Moralistic therapeutic deism and its doppelgangers *aren't* worth dying for. Young people give religion precisely the value they think it is worth, so when faith asks for nothing, this is exactly what it receives. Young people are correct that moralistic therapeutic deism helps them navigate our culture. What it doesn't do is change them, or make them part of a community that practices costly love, or engages in a story of divine love that overcomes existential shipwreck.

Teenagers know—better than we do—that when we ask them to follow Christ, we are asking them to enter dangerous territory. They know in their bones that true love is "to die for"; they get that this is the "ask" of real faith. For young people, Bonhoeffer's claim—that following Jesus is a bid "to come and die"—poses a very real threat.[23] Young people know that to claim Christ risks death on many fronts: Putting faith before friends risks social annihilation; choosing poorly-compensated work risks insecurity and discomfort; and joining ranks with the marginalized skewers visions of personal success that drive everything from the sports we play to the colleges we apply to.

Of course, to be liberated from someone else's idea of who we should be is also a disciple's great joy—but between here and there are countless rich young rulers who go away sad, unwilling to make the leap (Mark 10:22). The only way to protect young people from crushing risk in following Jesus is to abridge the story, to create a "safer" version that invites young people to be interesting without being odd, to be friendly without being foolish, to practice self-actualization instead of self-giving love. This, of course, begs the question: Have we offered them Christ at all?

2. The Culprit of Respectability:
The Professionalization of Youth Ministry

For most of the twentieth century, American youth ministry remained a regular but informal outpost of church work, a motley assortment of volunteers and teenagers who dabbled in religious practices and social activities in family rooms and church basements. The 1970s saw a shift. Churches, like American culture in general, scrambled to serve swelling numbers of teenagers (the "baby boom" of the 1950s and 1960s), creating a youth ministry market ravenous for resources. Thus, the youth ministry "industry" was born. Unlike Sunday schools' tendency to conform to the orderly grip of curriculum materials, youth ministries (almost universally experienced as "youth groups") reflected the whims, interests, and proclivities of well-meaning volunteers. By the 1970s, there was an urgent need for some common rules of engagement, less haphazard curricular resources, and more professional standards and practices.

To meet these needs, youth ministry entrepreneurs (and a handful of religious publishers) began turning out resources specifically aimed at youth groups. Churches began to create (poorly) paid positions for adults to work with young people; conferences began to recognize and serve "professional" youth ministers. Training opportunities for youth workers, in both formal and informal educational settings, began to proliferate. The presence of published resources and conferences in youth ministry meant something else, as well: For the first time, leaders could peer over their back fences to see what others were doing in the name of "youth ministry." It was a mixed view: toothpaste relays and subtle humiliations (mislabeled as "games") were as common as sermons and spaghetti dinners. In the early years especially, youth ministry resources amounted to an advice industry. Everyone was making it up on the fly, dispensing advice along the way.

Today's youth ministry industry is the result of those good intentions. The professionalization of youth ministry succeeded impressively—and problematically. By the early twenty-first century, youth ministry was supported by multiple publishers, degree programs, and professional and academic guilds conducting real research and scholarship. While youth ministry had long been taught in evangelical Christian colleges, Catholic and mainline Protestant theological education now joined the cause, partly because funding cuts left denominational youth ministries unmoored. Seminaries and divinity schools began to offer theological, not just educational and sociological, justifications for youth ministry; ministry with young people was declared a "vocation" like other forms of ministry. Celebrity influencers, publishers, certification programs, and the like all pressed toward "correct" (or at least "better") ways of doing youth ministry. As other forms of ministry had done decades earlier, youth ministry adopted professional standards and practices that made it more comparable to, and more credible with, other professions.

Interestingly, these support systems for youth ministry seemed to gel just as the National Study of Youth and Religion dropped its first report in 2009, challenging the long-held notion that doing youth ministry "better" was the solution to young people's fragile religious identities. The NSYR reframed the problem: Young people didn't hate religion; many churches offered strong youth ministries; even young people unimpressed with "church" felt positive about *their* churches. Tension over religion was not the problem—in fact, quite the opposite. The study revealed almost *no* tension around religion among the young people and parents surveyed. And for good reason. Churches were doing a fine job of what most adults wanted: socializing young people into a form of religious identity that was virtually indistinguishable from living a "good [American] life." Religion wasn't a problem. It just didn't *matter*.

Solving the Wrong Problems

The upshot of all this is that most of our efforts in youth ministry over the past few decades have been carefully calibrated to solve the wrong problems. I entered ministry in the 1980s, intent on helping stop the adolescent exodus from American church life. Like many of my peers, I assumed the answer was to "fix church" (i.e., make it more inviting/relevant/hospitable/contemporary—pick your adjective) for teenagers.

There was another reason for becoming a youth pastor: Youth ministry was one of the few places in the church where anybody was allowed to rearrange the furniture. I was a church camp kid; all of my most meaningful "God moments" as a teenager happened at camp, not in my local congregation. So my idea of "fixing church" meant making it look more like camp. (I wasn't alone: "Pass It On" and "El Shaddai"— camp songs of my youth—were in the United Methodist hymnal by the time I was an adult, and before long, hymnals themselves went out the window as the youth worship bands pulled together for retreats and youth conferences became commonplace in the sanctuary.) I viewed youth ministry as a laboratory where teenagers (and I) could "get away with" trying out new ways to worship and serve God. Like most of my colleagues in youth ministry at the time, I assumed that adolescents' disenchantment with religion could be solved if we could just *do ministry better*—and the place to figure out how to do that was in the unregulated space of the youth room.

We gave it our all. The adolescent exodus got worse.

It is now clear that we badly misread the situation. Our job was never to "fix church" (if we had paid more attention in theology classes, we would have known this). Youth ministry's professionalization over the past fifty years means that we *do church better* now than at any time in history. But it turns out that Christians needs less fixing and more following. By failing to place the oddity of Christ at the center of our work, by downplaying suffering love in the name of personal happiness, another gospel crept in. Tying ourselves to professionalization harnessed a trojan horse full of upward mobility assumptions. As youth ministry got "respectable" in schools, guilds, and professional organizations, we lost our willingness to let Jesus flip us on our heads. Youth ministry became a pillar of the right-side-up church, instead of a toehold for the upside-down reign of God.

Stranger Things: The Upside-Down Fellowship of *Agape*
In *The Upside-Down Kingdom,* Donald Kraybill describes the right-side-up church as one deluded by the very temptations that confronted Jesus: It is lured by security, beguiled by power, and tempted by cheap grace and superficial religion (represented in the temptation stories by the images of bread, mountain, and temple). After each conversation with the evil one, Jesus parries, providing a glimpse of the "upside-down kingdom" in response.[24] Turning stones to bread solves nothing if we are not really hungry for food; what we long for is God. Power is meaningless if it costs us our soul; God is the source of true power. Religion is impotent if we refuse to "get off our donkeys" and treat those dying in the ditch; God will not be a party trick who relieves us of responsibility.

Using Kraybill's framework, we could say that youth ministry is right-side up—it is not odd—when we give young people bread and circuses instead of the Bread of Life; when we turn loving actions into useful morality lessons or college resume fillers; and when we treat faith as a holy parachute, expecting Jesus to show up in our time of need without doing our part to show up for others (or for God). When we buy into these economic, political, and religious temptations, youth ministry participates in the right-side-up kingdom that Jesus decried.

The issue, of course, is how to cut the ropes that tie youth ministry to a right-side-up culture, and reclaim enough "wobble" in youth ministry for Jesus to turn us over. There is no model or curriculum for this. Our posture as much as our practice determines whether our ministries embalm young people in the fluids of self-fulfillment, or unbind them with the truth that sets them free. Most of our ministries do both; the idea is to tip the scale until down is up most of the time.

Kraybill's understanding of upside-down ministry is based in *agape:* love that is indiscriminate, bold, inconvenient, risky, time-consuming, expensive, excessive, revealing—and impossible. *Agape* is the love we long for but always fail to offer. And yet we have glimpsed it. There have been moments when we have experienced such love. There have been moments when we have participated in such love. We experience these moments as gifts, because they are. *Agape* is suffering love in the sense that it overwhelms us; it is self-loving ("love your neighbor as *yourself*") but also self-giving ("*love* your neighbor as yourself"). Such paradoxical love is possible only in Christ, named or unnamed, whose grace makes some human approximation of *agape* possible.

So where do we find the courage—and the grace—to challenge our culture's soul-killing economic, political, and religious habits that creep into youth ministry uninvited? A good first step is to stop equating youth ministry with church youth groups. While there is nothing wrong with a peer-group ministry, it is not equivalent to serving and bearing witness to Christ. A second step is to look for God's redemptive fingerprints: wherever *down is up, out is in, weak is strong,* or *death yields life,* something is happening that points to the inverting work of Christ. Taken together, it's worth recognizing what they have in common:

- **They don't shy away from divine or human suffering.** In fact, they lean into it. All of these ministries reject the division between server and served; all of them assume the contributions of young people who "stand with their backs against the wall," as Howard Thurman put it.[25] God suffers in solidarity with young people who struggle. Ministry is not the solution to their problems; rather, ministry mobilizes young people to create solutions marked by self-giving love.

- **They have a view from beneath.** Thanks to the fact that these ministries "see through" the eyes of young people on the margins, they notice details that those of us in our right-side-up pews tend to miss. The view from down under gives youth ministry a different angle and agenda, which offers two blessings. First, youth notice cultural deceptions quickly, since it is easier to see the cracks in the façade from below. Second, youth detect opportunities for the church that are only evident from under the table—making them "essential personnel" in any congregation.

- **They focus.** Instead of attempting to be all things to all people, upside-down youth ministries are biased toward particularity. Particularity is not a fast track to growth; these ministries can't be mass produced. Instead, they tend to focus on a particular struggle, experienced by particular teenagers. Then they saturate these young people with hope, homing in on one or two focused offerings (e.g., job training or contemplative prayer) that serve as signs of God's liberating grace for the young people in question. As these youth begin to recognize God in their midst, word goes out beyond the original group, drawing more and different young people to the ministry.

- **They don't need a youth group.** Upside-down youth ministries do not see themselves primarily as a church "club." Typically, they see their work as broader than a single congregation, and seek to transform communities or cultures, aiming outward, not inward. Upside-down youth ministries might be more aptly called "missional communities" than youth groups—bands of young people deployed by God for a particular purpose that they have discerned, or who choose to live in a way that bears witness to Christ's self-giving love in their community.

- **They aim for impact, not activity.** Upside-down youth ministry rescues us from our tendency to baptize busy-ness. Instead, youth in upside-down ministries discern divine action that is making a measurable difference in lives and communities, and join in. When Jesus turns us on our heads, *something changes.* We can point to what is different—not due to our impact, but to God's. The world is altered in ways that defy human nature: People who were first line up last, youth without power lead, greedy people share, lost people find their way, the faithless turn to prayer, the hopeless anticipate tomorrow.

Impact in ministry is not something we do "to" youth. It might be more accurate to say that impact is what God does to *us*, by binding us to the upside-down life of Jesus—which forever alters our view of reality. Whether youth ministry offers one activity or several is immaterial; what matters is participating in the *death-to-life difference* God makes in the world. Perhaps youth ministry offers young people access to mental health professionals—or maybe a garden. Perhaps it offers dignity through relationships—or through a job. Perhaps it counters failure with prayer—or maybe with worm farming that brings young people face-to-face with God's refusal to see waste the way we do (*see sidebar at the end of this chapter*). All of these are equally likely "youth activities" in upside-down youth ministry because they practice resurrection: They make a death-to-life difference. And by practicing resurrection, God gives you and me new life as well.

Twenty-First Century Youth Ministry: Making "Good Trouble"

The late congressman John Lewis, civil rights activist and the so-called "conscience of Congress," remembered being inspired by Rosa Parks and Martin Luther King to get into "good trouble, necessary trouble."[26] As a twenty-five-year-old activist, Lewis nearly lost his life in 1965's "Bloody Sunday" march across the Edmund Pettus Bridge in Selma, Alabama. Footage of Lewis being brutally beaten by police in the nonviolent protest turned the tables of the civil rights movement, galvanizing support for civil rights legislation in Congress. Good trouble—trouble that turns right-side-up complacency into upside-down witness—is often sacrificial trouble. For Lewis, it was also an act of faith. The stories of Jesus's composure while being tormented by his accusers were not far from these young protesters' minds. "We saw ourselves doing the work of the Almighty," Lewis told PBS in 2004. "Segregation and racial discrimination were not in keeping with our faith, so we had to do something."[27]

The post-pandemic era is a time of truth-telling for the church. Termites we have long denied in our religious infrastructure are now exposed. Economic models that have been faltering for decades are near collapse. Accustomed patterns of worship and community formation have been permanently disrupted. Heaven knows, we have no energy for a creative God right now. Everyone is exhausted. Right now we long for manageable dreams and closer horizons, smaller hopes and a smaller Christ, not because we are humbled, but because we are spent. We are too tired even to call "B.S."

But if the church is not willing to "turn the world upside down," as Paul's followers were accused of doing in Thessalonica, young people most definitely are. If anything is a recipe for good trouble, it's participating in *agape*—becoming agents of self-giving love in a self-fulfilling culture. And yet, anything less is not love. Anything less is not the church. With anything less, young people have every right to call B.S.

Kraybill reminds us that "The task of rebuilding the church is a new and urgent mandate of every generation."[28] He offers his description of *agape*—a snapshot of "re-weirdified" youth ministry:

We are the folks who engage in conspicuous sharing . . .
Our faith wags our pocketbooks.
We give without expecting a return.
We forgive liberally as God forgave us.
We overlook the signs of stigma hanging on the unlovely.
Genuine compassion for the poor and destitute moves us.
We look and move down the ladder.
We don't take our religious structures too seriously because we know
     Jesus is Lord . . . of religious custom.
We serve rather than dominate.
We invite rather than coerce.

Love replaces hate among us.
Shalom overcomes revenge . . .
We share power, love assertively, make peace.
We flatten hierarchies and behave like children…
Servant structures replace rigid hierarchies . . .
We join in a common life for worship and support.
Here we discern the times and the issues.
In the common life
    we discover the Spirit's direction for our individual and
corporate ministries.[28a]

In other words, upside-down youth ministry is the *church*—and no doubt about it, living like this will borrow trouble. Good trouble. Necessary trouble. Not B.S.

HOW I'M DOING THIS

DANIEL YODER

In my first decade of youth ministry, I knew what to do. The resources, cultural assumptions, and economic realities of my church matched those of the broader youth ministry world. Then my church started doing some hard work. We felt the Spirit calling us to look more like the community around us. To actually be part of that community.

The Spirit moved, and we changed. The average demographic of our church, located in Goshen, Indiana, shifted from white, affluent middle-class to lower-middle-class families with mixed documentation. And what I knew how to do no longer fit. I could lead a fantastic service and learning trip, but when families struggled for food and youth didn't have enough clothes to pack for a week, Jesus's geography-centric mission mandate struck me in a new way. Why was I leading youth to "Judea" and "Samaria" while keeping quiet about the injustice and lack of good news being shared in our "Jerusalem"?

I didn't know how to proceed in my increasingly intercultural congregation. So I drew on my childhood farm boy skills, learned a new trade, and developed something that fell in between a fundraiser and a small business. It's a weird experiment that lives at the intersection of worms, youth, food scraps, mentoring, vermicompost, employment, congregation, and community.

Casting Hope is a youth ministry initiative that offers curbside food scrap pick-up and vermicompost to our community, while offering skill development, employment, and discipleship to youth. Casting Hope attempts to do a lot of things, and do them at a worm's pace. It is upside-down ministry. It might look slow, sometimes pointless, and really vulnerable, but it is persistent, beneficial, and done in community.

Composting is the process by which food scraps and other organic matter decompose and the basic elements become rich, healthy soil.

It takes time, it takes work, things heat up, it can stink, and there is potential for greatness. All things that someone who has traveled in a van full of adolescents has experience with.

A few specific varieties of worms enter the mix in what's called vermicomposting. Composting worms love to live in community, eat decomposing food scraps, and leave behind compost gold called castings, or what we might refer to here as "W.S." Worms can eat their weight in food in two days, are packed with potential, have a small sense of physical space, and will do full-body convulsions when you try to remove them from their peers and observe them. Again, all things with which youth workers who interact with hormone-laden humans are experienced.

Ministry enters the picture through the context and method of our work. Whenever a Casting Hope employee and an adult mentor begin a job, we say our "work verse" together: "And whatever you do, in word or deed, do everything in the name of the Lord Jesus, giving thanks to God the Father through him" (Colossians 3:17, NRSV). When these words frame and motivate feeding and caring for worms, cleaning up other people's food scraps, designing and building compost bins, vehicle maintenance, accounting and invoicing, and a host of other tasks, youth experience and know that Christian vocation can include any interest and passion God might be leading them to.

Casting Hope has offered more growth and connection than I could have imagined for the young person who is our longest-running employee. Having a paycheck has opened the world of money management and savings for him, which has given him the ability to provide groceries for his family during economic downturns. He joyfully offers to buy me lunch. He knows the church and community better because he knows where people live, what they eat, and whether they drink tea or coffee. Our weekly hours on the pickup route give him space to ask questions about how the Central Mexican Catholicism his parents were rooted in interacts with American progressive Anabaptism, as well as pop culture in general. He has witnessed hidden potential, transformation, and resurrection within things overlooked by others, and has internalized that message for himself.

After six months of doing weekly curbside food scrap pick-up, I noticed this employee talking with a "customer" in the church hallway, then giving her a hug. He was wishing her a happy birthday. This youth, who had been too shy to talk to anyone, had taken the initiative to look through the church directory to find someone's birthday, approach her at church, and ask if he could give her a hug. This woman is a rather formidable retired seminary professor. But this young man saw her simply as a friend who wants to support him in a project rooted in resurrection. And it's hard to be intimidated by someone when you know where they live and what they eat. Our Casting Hope tagline is "Healing Goshen, One Worm at a Time." We are also seeing the transformation of humans, one person at a time.

Daniel Yoder has been in congregational ministry for nearly twenty years, and he and his wife, Talashia, have been on the pastoral team at College Mennonite Church since 2009. Outside of church and worms he enjoys raising two boys and caring for creation. For more on Casting Hope, go to www.castinghopegoshen.com.

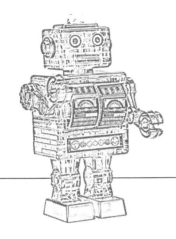

VIEW 2:
THE FUTURE IS YOUNG, URBAN, AND MULTIETHNIC

BY TOMMY NIXON

The future is young, urban, and multiethnic—and the future is here. I believe we are at the beginning of a new reformation in the Christian faith, and I believe youth ministry will play a crucial role in it. That is why you as youth workers are so important. In the next few pages, I want to share what I believe the future has in store for us in youth ministry and give two important keys to help all of us understand this new reality. Then, I'll offer three strategies to help you reach more youth with the gospel and disciple them in the way of Christ.

The Reality
1.2 million young people are leaving the church every year, according to the Pinetops Foundation and their Great Opportunity Report.[29] They are leaving because they are not compelled by the life they see professed Christians living and the gap between our theology and our praxis. We don't live out what we say we believe. To "love your neighbor as yourself" might seem like an overused Christian phrase, but we really stopped taking it seriously. In many ways it has become "love your neighbor into our Sunday morning service," and young people are not buying it anymore. There is a desperate need for the simple command to "love your neighbor as yourself" to be lived out as a picture of the kingdom of God and the heart of our King for this next generation—and yet, millions are leaving. Those leaving are not

people who are searching for God, but people who have experienced and heard the church's presentation of the gospel and rejected it. Though some of them might continue on a spiritual journey, they have chosen not to participate in the body of Christ. This disconnection and separation is detrimental to both the church and to those who have left it. We need each other if we are going to see and bring about the hope and healing this world desperately needs.

2020 was an incredibly difficult year, but it was also a catalyst to help us as the church come to grips with the things we need to address and change as we continue to profess Christ and his gospel. The continued good news is that 2020 challenged the church in significant ways and created glaring needs that we as the body of Christ are primed to address going forward—if we are awake to and aware of the opportunity.

Before we get to that, I want to make sure you understand where I am coming from. I will make this quick so we can get to the good stuff, but I think sharing more about my story will help frame my perspective.

I am mixed, with Filipino and European ethnicities, but I have blue eyes and light skin and no Filipinos are claiming *Pinoy* on me. I grew up in the African-American community. My father left and moved to Mexico when I was eleven and started another family, and I have Mexican siblings. I was saved at and went to a predominantly white megachurch growing up. Then in college, my friends and I started a nonprofit organization called Solidarity. With Solidarity, we moved into a first-generation Latino immigrant neighborhood. I lived in that area for fifteen years, and I was on the speaking team at a primarily Asian-American church for eight of them. My surroundings from childhood and the struggles I experienced all the way to the present would be labeled as "urban," with stints here and there in a privileged context and predominantly white spaces.

In 2018 I transitioned from the nonprofit I started as a young man into running Urban Youth Workers Institute, where our focus is on developing urban leaders. Through Urban Youth Workers Institute we recently filmed a panel of young people and asked them why they were leaving the church. Their responses were hard to listen to. These young people brought up all the things we in the church have avoided discussing for a long time: sexuality, race, economics, leadership, protests, politics, and my favorite one, hypocrisy.

Although these interviews were hard to hear, the young people's comments also resonated with me and my own wrestling with who we are as the church. Honestly it sounded a lot like what I was struggling with in the early 2000s when we started Solidarity. Leading up to that point, my friends and I went to a Christian university in Southern California. We had this sinking suspicion that there had to be more to following Christ than what we had experienced in our long lives to that point of twenty years. In every generation there is an angst against the establishment, and I was definitely angsty. The hypocrisy I saw and experienced in the church felt overwhelming at the time, but the grace of God helped me realize that before I started pointing the finger at the church's hypocrisy, I needed to remember that we are the living embodiment of the church. Partly in response to our feelings about the church as we'd experienced it, our focus with Solidarity was to love our neighbor as ourselves (Mark 12:31). The sixteen years I spent with Solidarity were an incredible experience in the kingdom of God. My partners and I made a ton of mistakes, but God, through our neighbors, crafted and shaped a theology and a praxis that I believe this next generation desperately needs.

Fast forward to now. It feels like the last twenty years of my life were preparation for all that shifted and changed in 2020. I work primarily with leaders of color and almost entirely with leaders in an urban setting. The pandemic and then the uprisings of the summer of 2020 were catalysts to the reality of the future. By 2045 the racial majority in this country will become the minority—but that shift happened in 2020 for those eighteen and under. The world is young, urban, and multiethnic or, in a global sense, non-white. Add to this the export of urban culture and hip-hop on a global scale and it is the urban youth worker who is now the key to the future of youth ministry and of the church.

Did I lose you right there? Stay with me. The world is shifting, and the center of power and culture is changing. We should all rejoice in this for two reasons. Number one, once we have recognized this shift, we have the opportunity to be proactive and not reactive. Instead of trying to hold on to what used to be, we can join with *Elohim* (Genesis 1), the strong Creator, and be part of creating something beautiful. Number two, the kingdom of God has always been more beautiful, vibrant, and effective from the margins. This is inherent in the strategy of the gospel. Christ was born into an oppressed people group, in an occupied country. Christ was an immigrant, lived in poverty, was homeless, was hated by the religious establishment, and was ultimately murdered by the state. Jesus rooted his mission on Earth with marginalized people (Luke 4:18-20). If you feel a sense of loss in this, I mourn with you, but I am also excited for you because when we recognize this truth, it puts all of us in a place of dependency on Christ as we die to ourselves and realign our hearts with God's.

This next generation wants and needs a gospel that makes sense in today's world. They need to understand how our belief in Christ engages in politics in a righteous way. How our theology affects our relationships and our sexuality. Young people ask, what does God have to do with injustice? Everything! That is part of the good news the difficult issues and upheavals of recent years have exposed. We have the opportunity to guide young angst toward a lived-out expression of the kingdom of God.

Key Number One:
Compassion—To Suffer With

This next generation cares a lot, about everything. One of the biggest challenges for the church in the last four years was that a majority of Christians seemed to care about the wrong things. Sound political? It is. Mostly because in the United States and inside the church we have bought into a false dichotomy of the right and the left. It has become easy for Christians to defer our values and our beliefs to a political party, even when that party does not uphold our beliefs in Christ. The right can be wrong but the left ain't right either. We must recognize that we can transcend those labels with the way of Christ. This becomes obvious when we reject the narrative and spin that both political parties place on these actual lives of people made in the image of God. If we believe in Christ the suffering servant, then we can agree that whether it is Black lives, children in cages, or the death of the unborn, Jesus has compassion.

Reread these passages about the suffering servant: Isaiah 42:1-4, Isaiah 49:1-6, Isaiah 50:4-7, and Isaiah 52:13-53:12. These vivid songs and prophecies of Christ are beautiful and compelling. They foretell a story that has since happened, and we are blessed to live in its aftermath. The idea that God would suffer with us and for us is exactly what this next generation desperately wants to know, but it's not what we have been living or communicating.

The witness of the church has been damaged. This damage has been compounded by the uprisings and protests of 2020, by the divisive state of our country, and by the continued politicization of evangelicals. When I have said this before I have been met with defensiveness—protestations about how a particular church is thriving, and theological arguments from both sides of the aisle about what we are currently living through being evidence of God's judgement.

But listen: 1.2 million. Young people. Are leaving. The church. Every year.

We have to do better. Gen Z cares deeply about the pain in the world and they need help and guidance to do something about it. Our difficult current circumstances present us as the church with the perfect opportunity to step up. The key to reaching this next generation is our ability to have compassion. And by compassion, I do not mean doing nice things for poor people. Compassion literally means "to suffer with." To suffer with is not necessarily "service to." You can serve someone without loving them, but you can't love someone without serving them. We do a lot of service, but we need to up our suffering game.

This is what I love so much about urban youth workers. They are adept at suffering and are experts in it because of the environments they grew up in. Poverty, fatherlessness, violence, substance abuse, and trauma were met with redemption through the gospel. It makes sense to me that God would raise up experts from these margins.

Through my work with Solidarity, I spent sixteen years learning how to suffer with others in the neighborhoods where we worked and lived. These were not Sunday and Wednesday gathering experiences, but daily lived-out expressions of the kingdom of God. We were neighbors and friends through celebration and mourning, parties and funerals. There was a shared experience of suffering. If my neighbor had roaches, *we* had roaches, and we worked on that roach problem together.

Here is what I learned: Ultimately, it wasn't about the suffering, it was about dependence on God. That's because when you put in the relational time and work to suffer with someone, it causes you to get in over your head so far that you realize that you can't save them. At that point it gets so difficult that you run back to God and complain, "I put in all this work and they are not responding!" or "this situation isn't getting any better!" This is when God speaks back and says, "I know. This is all I ever wanted, for us to be together" (John 15:4-8). God calls us into kingdom work not because he *needs* us but because he *wants to be with us*. Then he calls us to compassion—to suffer with—and that is what can help heal us of our independence.

The moments when we realize we are not the savior and we desperately need him are the continued intersections of salvation. Can you imagine if the church was known for how we suffered with others? Is that how you would describe the church now? It definitely is not how young people see it. Yet "suffering with" is at the core of who Jesus was and is. It is the mark that has characterized the church for thousands of years. We have been rejected by this next generation for not living into Christ's compassion.

During the COVID pandemic you may have lost friends or family to arguments about masks, vaccines, political candidates, worship services, etc. In the midst of this upheaval, I was reminded of something I find baffling: people who claim Christ but deny the pain of large groupings of other people. People who seemed to show an overwhelming lack of care. Whether it was in response to police violence, kids in cages, or mass incarceration, the denial of people's pain is so un-Christlike. This denial is the opposite of compassion. It is anti-gospel. And young people are watching. They are noticing. They are seeing, again and again, that very often the world's systems and the church have no answer to the things young people care about.

For just one example, let's think about racism. You know the world's general response to racism? It's something like this: "Hey, be aware enough so that you don't come off racist." In other words, say the right things, post the right things, and you get the social pass. But this attitude never deals with the sinfulness of one group of image bearers believing they are superior to another group of image bearers and upholding a system that benefits one over the other. (If you don't believe there is a system, read this chapter again. Do the work to investigate what young people care about and how the gospel is so relevant to issues such as systemic racism.)

At this point you might be feeling defensive, but self-examination and critique are at the core of what we as Christ followers all believe. Romans 3:23 says "All have sinned and fallen short of the glory of God." If we are honest, we often feel like some have fallen a lot shorter than others. But the deeper truth is that we all come to Christ because we realize that we have deficiencies, that we need a savior. That we were wrong. Spiritual formation is an ongoing process. We can see where we are now as an opportunity to press into God even more—or we can be defensive, keep doing what we are doing, and continue to watch the mass exodus of young people from the church. It is the art of self-examination in relationship to God's righteousness and Word that leads us to dependence on and depth with God.

Key Number Two: Reframing the Gospel

The second key to helping youth workers right now is reframing the gospel. I don't mean that we need to change it. I mean we need to express the truth of the gospel in a way that recaptures and communicates the power of what Christ has done for us and how it changes things in the here and now.

When I first moved into the neighborhood where we were running after-school programs through Solidarity, a local church gave me something called an evange-cube. It was a Rubik's Cube-looking box that flipped this way and that way to reveal different parts of the gospel story. In one of the panels you could create there was heaven on top, Christ's hand reaching out to another hand in the middle, and hell on the bottom. The message was simple: You don't want to go to hell, do you? You want to someday go to heaven, right? Then Jesus is the way.

We need to rethink this type of approach. In our efforts to give a quick and easy presentation of the gospel, the church has boiled it down into a two-minute explanation with an ask at the end. Granted, I have sometimes watched the Holy Spirit move and bring people to Christ through these kinds of talks. However, I would push back against the assumption of some youth workers that our goal is simply to get young people to say a specific prayer. We need to challenge the overall strategy here, because it's not working for enough people.

We are communicating with the most informed generation ever. They have access to endless information. What they need is wisdom and guidance. And for too many young people, the gospel they have witnessed is not the good news for the poor, release for the prisoner, sight for the blind, and freedom for the oppressed (Luke 4:18), even though this is literally what Jesus said as he started his work here on Earth. Those words of Jesus are the truths we need to proclaim. Romans 10:14-17 says,

> How, then, can they call on the one they have not believed in? And how can they believe in the one of whom they have not heard? And how can they hear without someone preaching to them? And how can anyone preach unless they are sent? As it is written, "How beautiful are the feet of those who bring good news!" But not all the Israelites accepted the good news. For Isaiah says, "Lord, who has believed our message?" Consequently, faith comes from hearing the message, and the message is heard through the word about Christ.

It strikes me that Paul writes in verse 16 that the Israelites heard, but did not obey. These words are an indictment on us as the church. Our job is not just preaching, but showing obedience to what is heard (James 1). This isn't the social gospel, and this isn't a debate between Rob Bell and Francis Chan on hell. This is about our call to actually live out the teachings of Jesus. To be formed into a peculiar, radical group of disciples who have given their lives for Christ. This is what will give young people the sense of purpose they so desperately want. Too often we as Christians have thwarted our true purpose, behaving as if it's enough to have a sense of comfort and easy belief. That is not even close to enough.

In Colossians 1:25, Paul writes, "I have become [the church's] servant by the commission God gave me to present to you the word of God in its fullness..." Paul is referring specifically here to Gentiles being included in the promise of the gospel, but the verse also seems applicable as we think about the future of youth ministry. We have not displayed the fullness of the Word of God in our world.

I am on several youth ministry Facebook pages where there are tens of thousands of youth workers posting daily. The posts I see most often are about what games they should play with their youth, what appropriate movies they could show, what fun events they could do, and how to set up their youth rooms. The thinking behind these posts is that if we can get young people interested enough to show up at our services, they can then hear the gospel, and we therefore are doing what Paul talked about in Romans 10. But the truth is, it's not working.

We are often limiting the faith to creating a youth-friendly atmosphere where we share about not going to hell and making it to heaven—and this is a central part of what's driving millions to leave the faith and the church. We need to move from conveying that salvation comes only through church participation into inviting young people to participate in God's kingdom and movement in the world. We need to convey that the kingdom is now and not yet. We need to share that the good news of the gospel is not that you make a decision for Christ and then have to wait to die to experience his goodness—but rather that you can experience the kingdom of God right now.

These truths are so important for young people to hear and understand. Think about their world in the 2020s. All of the adults can't figure out how to deal with the issues we are facing. There is massive disagreement over how to deal with the pandemic and the adults in charge can't or won't find ways to work together or agree on much of anything. Young people know they are inheriting massive amounts of debt and systemic injustice, and they are facing a global recession. And what are they supposed to do about it?

What happens too often is we as youth workers come along and respond to all of this simplistically by saying that Jesus is the way. Young people know they are being placated. They hear you, but their questions are still there: "Okay, but what about all these issues?" Too often we continue to ignore the questions completely, saying something that boils down to "Accept Christ, live a moral life, and then when you die you'll get to go to heaven." But young people are not buying it. This way of thinking completely misses the abundant life that Jesus talks about in John 10. When we are most concerned with what games to play and what movies we can show and giving a simplified message about salvation, it's no wonder we are aren't capturing young people's attention in the long term.

The next generation deeply desires identity, purpose, and belonging. We can meet them in this. Where we are at our best is when we are on mission and purpose. We have the opportunity to give young people something worth fighting for, not the status quo Christianity so many of them have rejected.

So how do we do all of this?

I have three bold ideas to help you reach more youth with the gospel and disciple them in the way of Christ. As you read, remember that the world has changed and we need to rethink reaching this next generation. When the strategies of old are simply not working, it is time to be bold and try new things for the sake of the gospel and the church.

Content and Community...Online

In Matthew 28, Jesus commanded his followers to go and make disciples. So, the disciples went, all over the world. The early apostles went where the people were: temples, markets, homes, synagogues, meeting halls, and judicial courts. We have reversed that. Where once disciples *went*, we now say *come*. Come to our service, come to our church building, come to our event. There is nothing inherently wrong with this, but it does beg the question: What do we do when young people stop coming? That's when we have to remember that we are called to *go* to them. So, where are they?

They are in the digital space. I know you know that. In fact I know that when the pandemic started you tried really hard to set up Zoom and to connect with teens online. I also know that once teenagers started having to spend six hours online for school every day, a lot of your engagement dropped off. I get how the digital space could be off-putting to you, and sometimes to them. But it's not going away.

So, this is bold idea number one: You need to play more video games. Stick with me. The video game industry made almost $180 billion last year. That is more than the entire global film industry and North American sports combined.[30] And what's incredible is that even when your teenagers can't hang with another Zoom call, they will jump on their favorite game with their friends for hours after school.

I recently started playing online with a junior higher I have known since birth. His mom grew up with us in the neighborhood, but this guy has barely spoken to me in his twelve years of life. When we connected on this game for a couple of hours, he talked my ear off. I have never heard him so animated.

There is a principle here that is so important for us to remember: We need to have a context for a relationship. In other words, there needs to be a reason to be together with young people. It used to be that church in and of itself was the reason, though we all know some of the motivations for why people came were not great: parents made them, the fear of hell, some sense of obligation, or because their friends did. (All of this also helps explain why once young people graduate, they don't stay engaged in the local church or walking with Christ.) Church alone is no longer reason enough. So, we need to create a context for relationship. If they are not coming to us anymore then we have to go to them. Now you can sit there and be like, "I hate video games, that's so lame." I said the same thing about social media to one of my leaders who was in her early twenties. She looked at me and said, "You don't think that the Apostle Paul would have loved Twitter and used it for God's glory?" I playfully told her to shut up, but she was right. My kids are online playing video games, so that's where I am, too.

Maybe for the teenagers you know video games are not the way to connect. Regardless, it is true that if we don't press into the digital world then we are refusing to go where young people are. Bobby Lopez, one of the leaders Urban Youth Workers works with, runs PassionLA in East LA, a ministry that targets at-risk urban young people. He saw the COVID pandemic coming a couple of weeks before most people did. And because he saw it coming, he stopped his programs and focused on creating content for TikTok and Instagram. His ministry simply took what they were doing in discipling teens in East LA and put it into 59-second clips. Sometimes this meant he would take one sermon and break it down into fourteen pieces. Passion LA used teens to produce all of the content, which combined leadership development, discipleship, evangelism, and outreach, all in 59-second increments. Teens and adults would share their testimonies in under a minute, and they were powerful. These were real people talking about real life, real problems. One video reached 2.8 million views, and they had 5 million total views of their other videos, more than 1.5 million likes, and about 123,000 followers. Bobby says, "Those likes, views, and follows represent people who are hearing about God's goodness and being guided by our relationship health curriculum. As well as replying to comments and prayer requests, the PassionLA team meets with people they connect with. We are now working on the other part of our strategy to help connect and disciple these people we are connecting with."

Content can create community. One of the content pieces PassionLA makes is "Dad and Mom Advice," where Bobby and his wife, Mayra, share bits of wisdom from their experience with Christ restoring them after growing up in toxic and traumatic environments. PassionLA has young people all over the country messaging about how this series has impacted their lives. Social media has given so much opportunity to share the truth of the gospel and has created a sense of community through shared suffering and experience.

While I've included numbers above to show the scale of what can happen, the truth is that it doesn't matter if you have thousands of followers or you are engaging with twelve teenagers online. You can use social media to share the gospel through your own life, your leaders' lives, and the lives of the young people you're ministering to.

In the summer of 2020, our organization partnered with some of our friends at nonprofits Love Thy Nerd and Satellite Gaming to create a training for youth workers called Developing Digital Disciples, a framework and a how-to for engaging young people digitally. Our team broke it into four phases: Find Affinity, Create Proximity, Grow Influence, and Create Lasting Impact.[31] Again, the important and beautiful part of what's happening here is that when we engage online, we can create our own context for relationship. You might not be into video games, but I guarantee someone in your youth group is. Find ways to create or jump into a digital context for relationship, whether it's online gaming, social media, or YouTube content creation. Search out where your teenagers are finding context and community online, and look for how you or your ministry can be part of it. Even if you're horrible at all things digital, these young people are worth it and they desperately need what you have to give.

Every Church a Community Center

A friend of mine was on city council in Santa Ana, California. During his time in that role, he had a vision: every church a community center. I loved that. Imagine all the church buildings in your community filled with neighbors experiencing the kingdom of God as they are welcomed in and given what they need to thrive. This brings me to **bold idea number two: Run a community center out of your church.** Or go partner with someone already doing something similar at their church or other location. Make creating a space for the community a core part of your work with your youth and for your youth.

Why should we be offering our church spaces as community centers? For one, on church properties there is so much wasted physical space between Monday and Saturday. Even large churches with a lot of programs during the week are mostly offering those programs to the people who are already part of the church. What if we opened up our buildings in new ways, for people outside our congregations to use as well?

I was encouraged when so many churches used their properties to provide pandemic relief. From simple food distribution centers to helping neighbors prepare their children for online learning to providing information for neighbors who speak a different language, I saw the church step up. That was beautiful, and I hope it won't stop there. How else can we be creative with the assets God has given us? Even if you don't have a building, keep looking for ways to call your teenagers to change the world starting with what is around them. This is crucial for their development, and it's what this generation wants to be a part of.

My life was changed as a ninth grader when one of our youth leaders took us to meet and pray for the neighbors around our church. At the time I went to a megachurch in the middle of Pasadena, California, but right around the church there were areas of poverty. My youth leader took us door to door to meet our neighbors. We introduced ourselves and asked simple questions to get to know each other. It was powerful, and I connected with the people we met. There were mutual experiences of suffering. I knew what poverty felt like and what it was like to be in a house without a father. I had grown up in neighborhoods and schools like these. Meeting our church's neighbors shaped me, and showed me that I had the agency to continue stepping into what God is doing in the world, even when it was just across the street.

Six years later I was interning in the youth ministry of a large church in Costa Mesa, California. One year we came up with the idea to do reverse trick-or-treating. We went to all the neighbors around the church office and handed out candy. That neighborhood, however, was nothing like the make-up of our church. The neighborhood was predominantly Latino, and the church was this up-and-coming hipster church in Orange County. Even so, I was reminded of my first experience visiting neighbors with my youth group six years earlier. After our trick-or-treating experience I asked if we could start reaching out into the neighborhood consistently. I was told no: that was not part of the values of the church.

I was so put off by that answer that I went and did it myself, starting Solidarity. My deep prayer, though, is that churches would be open to their neighbors and active in their neighborhoods. I pray to see the church be a hub for the community.

This next generation wants to change the world. They yearn to feel a sense of purpose. So help them start doing that exactly where they are. To begin, simply ask what is God up to in your community. Invite your teenagers, staff, and volunteers to brainstorm. Where is good happening, and how can you join in on it? Sometimes an opportunity will present itself when God wants to do something new. I experienced this with Solidarity, when brainstorming, praying, and walking through the neighborhood led very quickly to the man who ran a community center giving us keys to the building to start running an after-school program. So ask yourself: What are the wants and needs of your community and neighbors? How can you join in on what their hopes are for their community? What can you do that lives beyond the Sundays and Wednesdays?

The community centers we ran through Solidarity were places where people felt safe, where they were listened to, and where they found resources, a network of relationships, and opportunities. Can you imagine if that's how the church was described by this next generation? When we connect the church and community, it's powerful. It is how a kid like me who had no money could grow in experience and end up traveling the world and fundraise millions of dollars for kingdom work. It's how I saw healthy marriages modeled. When we start engaging in what God is up to outside of the church's four walls, we become the answers Gen Z so desperately needs to see, experience, and join in on.

Mentoring

If you look up "mentoring Generation Z," you'll uncover a ton of stats for businesses about mentoring this generation. For instance, this one: 60% of Gen Z want to make a difference in the world[32] and "69% of Gen Z job seekers wouldn't take a position with a company that has a bad reputation. How you show up for your workforce and your community matters."[33]

I will make the connection explicitly here if you haven't already: If this next generation won't take a job because of a company's reputation, what are the implications for the church? With all the flak that the church takes, sometimes deservedly, church history does show the transformative power of the gospel to make the world better and Christ's name known. But every time we trade our identity to align ourselves with any power structure other than Christ, horrible things happen. Unfortunately, it is that collective memory and history that has imprinted itself on this young generation.

I believe we can change that.

This is bold idea number three: Your youth ministry should be a mentoring program. This is not a ploy to get more youth on Wednesday nights. I am saying run a legit mentoring program based in your church. Offer it to students at your local schools and colleges. Put time, energy, and money into it.

The strategy here is twofold. You currently have a lot of churched adults in your Sunday services who desperately need to live out the theology they hear and sing every Sunday. The beautiful thing is that there is also is a generation of young people who want and need mentors. If we take our calling from Christ seriously and we invest in mentoring relationships, everybody wins.

Discipleship is a dynamic process: We need those we disciple just as much as they need us. I've learned this from experience. When we first started Solidarity, I really thought I was bringing Jesus to the neighborhood. I was hanging out with kids at the community center, walking the neighborhood, showing kids the evange-cube, and asking if they knew about Jesus. One kid said, "Yeah, Ms. Lynn has been teaching us the Bible for the last eight years out of that apartment right there."

My first reaction was, *"Yeah but did she teach it to you right? Did she use an evange-cube?!"* I didn't say that, but I thought it. So I went and met with Lynn to see if I could join her in what she was doing. I hoped we could partner in ministry. She was so happy Solidarity was there— but not for the reason I hoped. In actuality, Lynn had been loving this community for eight years but felt very little support from her church. By the time we showed up she was glad to be able to pass off this calling knowing that someone could continue the work. She was gone in the next month. She wanted to be a mentor and a support, but her church wasn't supporting and encouraging her as she loved her community.

Though we were unable to partner with Ms. Lynn, for the next six years we worked and walked daily with the families and neighbors in the Garnet neighborhood in Fullerton, California. Then the recession of 2008 hit and donations started to plummet. It got to a point where we couldn't pay anybody on staff and had spent all our savings to keep things going. As a staff and community, we would take whoever's check matched the amount that was needed for costs, cash it, and pay each other's bills. Finally, there was nothing left, and we had a housing payment coming up. Those of us who lived together were sitting in my living room when we heard a knock on the door. It happened to be two guys named Sergio (yes, two Sergios). They explained that they knew we were struggling, and they had gone around the neighborhood and collected cash to support us—cash collected for our nonprofit from the people we had come to "save." Our friends and neighbors were really struggling, and yet the people we had come to serve were serving us. I thought I came to save the neighborhood, but it was Jesus through the neighborhood who saved me.

That experienced shaped my understanding of God's strategy and sense of what he is up to. It displays what the church is and could be. I think this is the beauty of mentoring. Christ calls those of us who are youth workers to care about pastoring and also about creating connections between the adults in our churches and the teenagers in our churches and communities. That's how all of us come to a deeper knowledge of Christ. This is how we transform youth groups from being these strange add-ons to a church and integrating them into the life of the overall body.

I can imagine your concerns: "My pastor won't go for this." "I can barely get volunteers as it is." "This all sounds way too big." I know. That's all probably true. So, start with one. One person who wants a mentor. Ask questions, see where your mentee wants to grow, teach them skills, invite them into your life. Let them see how you live for Christ. Then share that story with someone else and invite them to be a mentor, and someone else to be a mentee. Learn from the failures and pay close attention to what God is up to in your own life.

Imagine if churches all over the country saw mentoring as a means of discipleship for their own people. Imagine them giving time, energy, and money, and networking to help out young people. Imagine a whole generation of young people who were mentored by Christ-centered adults. Imagine the impact of these relationships.

Now What?

Here is the beautiful thing. The three ideas I've given in this chapter can combine into an overall strategy. You can start with content and community online, move into being a community hub where you invite your current youth on mission and welcome new people in, and then you can take it the next step into a mentoring program. This is a natural progression, one that will give you the time and the space to work on and grow. Your youth group will grow, and your church will have an amazing opportunity to disciple and be discipled. Each strategy can also help bring diversity into your church and will help you grow in ways that you cannot achieve in a homogenous setting. The more we press into this new world, the more we will reflect God's kingdom. The future is here.

HOW I'M DOING THIS

VANESSA CRUZ

One day, I was awakened by my phone ringing at 7 o'clock in the morning. I heard a young person trying to catch her breath from crying as she painfully shared, "My dad was just picked up by ICE. He's gone. He was just taking out the trash before taking us to school." This family's world was turned upside down within seconds, and the first person this high schooler called was her youth pastor.

This became an opportunity for the church to step into this family's pain and trauma, and the journey of immigration they were about to embark on. That is exactly what we did. The church supported, encouraged, prayed, resourced, and did everything we could to let this family know that we were not going anywhere and that we were with them. This is the gospel lived out in my context.

Youth ministry in an urban setting has always been about the church stepping into and engaging in the realities of our community and families. Realities such as families being torn apart, and youth living in fear that one day their parents might not pick them up from school or come back home. The reality that our youth are witnessing violence in their communities and in their homes. The reality that racism is not just something to be "aware" of, but that it is what our youth experience firsthand, that it is their norm. That human trafficking happens in our very own cities, and is something the youth in our communities are vulnerable to and at risk of. That mental health issues are prevalent and yet very little support is available.

In an urban context, the church is naturally inclined to being part of the community and not the other way around. We've learned we just *have* to be. And this, I'm convinced, will become more normal and needed for churches in all contexts in the decades to come. As Tommy wrote in his chapter, using our church's physical spaces as assets and resources for the families we serve can be a core part of our work with and for our teenagers.

In my context, we have the privilege of being known in our community as a church *for* the city. Our greatest pride is when we are called to be part of conversations where we can collaborate with others to best serve the needs in our community. Recently, one of our neighborhood associations saw a need when youth were hanging out on Friday evenings and getting into trouble. The association invited our church into the conversation and together with other organizations, we came up with a skateboarding event hosted at our church parking lot. This created a space for the youth in our community to skate and have a safe place to hang out on those nights.

In order to best serve youth, we have no choice but to step into and engage in their world. We are doing them a disservice if we think that them coming to us is enough. No, we have to get past the surface level of youth ministry. Part of that means being part of the pain, the mess, the hurt, the trauma. We have to be willing to be in the tension of it all. This is what it means to live out the gospel. Jesus never promised that it would be easy but he did command us to love our neighbor (Mark 12:31).

Tommy reminds us of Jesus's command to "go and make disciples" (Matthew 28). Like the apostles, we should be going where the people are. This has become the core of who we are and want to be known for as a youth ministry. In our context, the first thing we did was get rid of our weekly big youth night gatherings. We decided that what was more important was to go to teenagers and begin what we call "life groups." Instead of our volunteer leaders committing to a weekly youth night program, they would now commit to leading a life group with a handful of youth every week. Life groups met at the park, at some of our church families' homes, at In-N-Out, in coffee shops, and, eventually in 2020, via Zoom.

Our "big" youth night gatherings transitioned to once a month, and life groups became the heart and focus of youth ministry. We stepped into and engaged in their world. Life groups are where youth began to truly feel seen and heard, and they allowed our leaders to be intentional about discipleship.

Student life groups not only became the vehicle for us to meet youth where they are but allowed us to shift and empower our young people to go and live out their faith. Our middle school life group met at a local boba spot, where they were approached by another middle schooler who wanted to know what they were up to. She was intrigued and was immediately invited to join their group. This young girl would have never experienced this faith community if it weren't for them being out in the neighborhood.

Now is the time to not only see the reality of what young people are living, but step into and engage in their world. As we do just that it will help us to care about what they care about. Is it possible that God could be using Generation Z to reveal what grieves his heart in order to make a difference in our world today? Like Tommy shared, the gospel is the answer this generation is looking so hard to find and experience for themselves. You and I have been chosen to give them something worth fighting for as we step into and engage in our communities.

Vanessa Cruz serves as the Director of Student Ministries at Revive Church in Long Beach and El Monte, California. She works with foster and at-risk youth and is passionate about empowering young people to achieve and obtain ALL that God has for them. She graduated with her Master's in Social Work from California State University of Long Beach, has her B.A. from Biola University, and is a Certified Urban Youth Worker through UYWI's 90 Degrees program. In her free time, she loves traveling and eating good food with close friends and her husband.

VIEW 3:
THE CURIOUS CASE
OF THE DISAPPEARING
YOUTH WORKER

BY MARK DEVRIES

Meet the Mad Scientist of Youth Ministry

There's a good chance that most youth workers in America have been touched by the work of my friend Rick Lawrence, even if they never learned his name. If you've ever read the annual salary survey for youth workers from *Group* magazine (which he edited for decades), if you've ever heard of Simply Youth Ministry or *Jesus-Centered Youth Ministry*, if you've ever attended one of Group's countless trainings or used one of their curriculum resources, you've been impacted by Rick.

Some of us have been fortunate enough to watch Rick in action and to see Jesus in whole new ways through Rick's remarkably engaging teaching style, one that makes it virtually impossible to remain a disengaged spectator. Rick is my favorite youth ministry mad scientist.

He has been tinkering around in his youth ministry laboratory for decades now, running hundreds of experiments, seeking to discover the most effective means of catalyzing spiritual transformation in youth (and their leaders). When the rest of us were staying in the safe lane of preparing and giving sage-on-the-stage messages and leading groups with astoundingly predictable methods, Rick was disarming every group he led, with invitations beginning, "Try something with me."

But beyond his impact on youth ministry, Rick is one of the kindest and most humble, creative, and wise Christian men I have ever known. When we are both at national youth ministry gatherings, I make a point of scheduling time with Rick, just to listen in on his ridiculous attention to God and to the Spirit's unfolding work in his life and work. I always walk away better.

Over the past few years, when I have asked Rick what is stirring his cocoa, he doesn't talk about a single thing that is part of his actual job as an author, speaker, and ministry leader. Instead, he brings up this little "experiment" he's been working on for the past six or seven years.

Most weeks of the year, one night each week, you'll find Rick and his wife, Bev, at home, surrounded by twenty or so teenagers and young adults. Like I said, this is not part of his day job. He's not doing this as a representative of his church. He hasn't been paid a single dime for the thousands of hours he's dedicated to this experiment.

Over the past seven years, Rick and Bev have developed what they call a "Vertical/Horizontal" strategy, using a model that, amazingly, allows every young person in the room to engage, no matter how old they are or their maturity level (the age span of the gathered group can include middle schoolers through post-college young adults). The vertical focus is unapologetically "Jesus-centered,"[34] making explicit the priority of growing an intimate appreciation for and relationship with Jesus. The horizontal focus is fundamentally "discovery-based"—both relational and improvisational—using mixed conversation groups of two, three, four, and the whole group, with Rick creating, then debriefing, experiences, projects, and stories, including film clips and video content, as catalysts for conversation.[35]

Might Rick and Bev, I wonder, be giving us a glimpse into the future of youth ministry?

Rick argues, quite persuasively, that the kind of volunteer work he's doing in his living room or basement (or his backyard or on Zoom) takes seriously the fact that Gen Z teenagers want to be "a part of a conversation, not passive consumers of a monologue." He points to patterns that social scientists are seeing in this emerging generation, specifically that they:

- are entrepreneurial by nature
- insist on hands-on participation in their learning (internships)
- want to be both the artist and the subject of the art
- want to be participants in social activism, not observers of it
- are "micro-interactors"—trained to quickly create and deliver their responses
- will pay attention to marketing if they help produce it
- want "authentic" experiences, not scripted ones[36]

If you're like me, you might just read through that list and say, "Wait, I'M looking for the same kinds of things!"

What if Gen Z is ushering us into ways of doing youth ministry that we know in our souls will be much more likely to produce lifelong disciples? What if their slowness to embrace the ways we've been doing youth ministry for decades might just loosen our death grip on the models that *used to* work? What if their passive resistance (i.e., not showing up) has the potential to push us to see discipleship as more than delivering well-packaged content? What if the backbone of the future of youth ministry belongs to

- those who don't get paid?

- those whose identities (and livelihoods) don't depend on maintaining the status quo?

- those who don't care about building big crowds?

- those focused on experimental spaces where young people cocreate their identities, their faith, and their callings?

The Shifting Landscape of Youth Ministry

The role of full-time youth pastor is not quite in danger of extinction, but it probably does belong on the endangered species list.

And that shift might not be such a bad thing.

As a refresher, here's how we got to where we are:

The 1970s saw the rise of the Youth Ministry Industrial Complex. Since then, youth ministry has blossomed into a dizzying array of networks, products, services, and assumptions. While the Youth Ministry Industrial Complex has disproportionately impacted white, suburban churches and schools, its (often unspoken) assumptions have spread widely across an extensive variety of denominations, theological tribes, ministry contexts, and very different academic institutions.

By the 1980s, it had become standard operating procedure for churches with over 100 people in worship (and many churches that were much smaller) to include the position of youth pastor (a.k.a. "youth director," "youth minister," or "youth worker") among its essential personnel. While many churches could only afford part-time youth workers, almost every church that could imagine a future for itself had hired someone to lead its ministry for teenagers.

The methods, assumptions, connections, and resources of the Youth Ministry Industrial Complex bloomed through the delivery system of an exploding number of youth ministry conventions. Some were tribal, anchored in specific denominational, geographical, or theological traditions; others cut delightfully across traditional boundaries and brought youth workers of different stripes from all around the country, sometimes all around the world, for the sake of the next generation.

At their height, these conventions attracted thousands youth workers, sometimes even tens of thousands. The result was an amorphous fusion of friendships and ideas that bridged walls that had, up to that point, been almost impossible to scale.

By the early 2000s, youth ministry had become an established profession, with more and more colleges and seminaries placing an intentional focus on the next generation, with majors, concentrations, and even PhDs in this rapidly growing field.[37] These streams came together around a single youth ministry assumption that has been more widely embraced than any other: The dependence on paid youth workers as the essential delivery mechanism for effective youth ministry.[38]

Though it may feel disheartening to read, I believe that the profession of youth ministry has now hit its peak and is due for a steady, if not precipitous, decline over the coming decades. After years of advocating for the expansion of the profession of youth ministry, I get no pleasure in predicting its decline. After all, I spent over thirty years as a full-time youth pastor. My son and daughter are both full-time youth pastors (and I like the idea of my grandchildren getting to eat).

But this is a perspective that more and more youth ministry influencers are beginning to accept. In a recent blog post, Dan McPherson identified this growing recognition when he wrote,

> In my reading and observation I've seen a growing popular opinion that full-time youth workers will soon become a thing of the past. As mega-churches become fewer and churches' budgets dwindle, youth workers will either be part-time or lay volunteers. As a full-time youth worker who wants to serve in youth ministry for a long time, this is a little disconcerting to me, but I do tend to agree with the majority however and see this as a dying trend.[39]

As I consider the shifting landscape of youth ministry and take a realistic look at the past twenty or thirty years, I have trouble reaching a different conclusion. Here are four reasons why:

1. Financial Realities

It is highly likely that by the time we hit 2050, only a fraction of the current number of full-time, church-based youth ministry positions will even exist. It won't be from a lack of desire; it will be from a lack of cash.

Even a cursory review of generational giving patterns reveals that boomers (born between 1946 and 1964) and traditionalists (born before 1946) account for a much bigger slice of the charitable pie and are *much* more oriented to giving to institutions (like churches) than are the generations that follow. In fact, in 2019 these groups accounted for a whopping 69% of all charitable giving.[40]

It's not that younger generations are not generous; it's just that they a) have less disposable income than their elders and b) are much less *institutionally* generous. Emerging generations tend to give to causes that *move them* much more than to institutions that *expect from them.* Though younger generations may volunteer more of their time than boomers, there is no denying that churches have built their youth programs and staffing models on boomer and traditionalist giving patterns.

By the time the average church figures out that their one-size-fits-all, duty-driven approach to unified giving just doesn't consistently work for those under sixty, many churches will find themselves having to radically readjust their budgets on the fly. Some will simply close their doors. For churches that stay around, it is not difficult to imagine that one of the first budget adjustments to be made will involve the position of a full-time youth pastor.

The ironic news is that, in the next thirty years or so, boomers and traditionalists will be passing along something in the neighborhood of $59 trillion in assets to subsequent generations.[41] Gen Xers and millennials could become the most significant philanthropists in history. Sure, some of that money will be going to churches. But unless something changes dramatically, the typical church will likely face a predictable decline, brought on by an acutely decreasing stream of resources.

The real tragedy is that we can see this coming. We've got time. But most churches are so caught up in the tsunami of business as usual that very few are paying attention to the financial cliff in the not-too-distant future. Fewer still have even considered alternative economic models, much less begun the process of planning for a very different financial future.

2. Impact Realities
Whether it's Sticky Faith or the National Study of Youth and Religion or other large-scale research projects, what has become clear is that the traditional model of youth ministry *may have* successfully created energy, attendance, and programs. What it hasn't done so well is create lifelong disciples of Jesus.

The Barna Group has summarized this pattern, repeating—perhaps with different numbers—the refrain that has become the ominous soundtrack most youth workers hear playing in their heads:

> Millennials are leaving the church. Nearly six in ten (59%) young
> people <u>who grow up in Christian churches</u> end up walking away,
> and the unchurched segment among Millennials has increased in
> the last decade from 44% to 52%, mirroring a larger cultural trend
> away from churchgoing in America. When asked what has helped
> their faith grow, <u>"church" does not make even the top 10 factors</u>.[42]
> (emphasis mine)

One unanticipated consequence of highly gifted, professional youth
workers is that we have successfully socialized many of our youth into
believing that the most faithful expression of Christian discipleship
is following their friends like lemmings. What is becoming clear is
that helping youth become enthusiastic spectators of someone else's
impressive faith does not yield the lifelong fruit any of us are really
looking for.

Sadly, in our current model, youth workers don't get compensated for
cultivating lifelong disciples. We get compensated for motivating young
people to come to church meetings. In what has become the "normal"
model, it is not uncommon for youth workers to also get compensated
for filling in gaps in the church, work that often has little to no impact
on developing lifelong faith in teenagers.

If a church is "fortunate" enough to get a youth center, the youth pastor
can easily become a facilities manager. When the church realizes how
few young adults are now in the church, it has become common to add
"and Young Adults" to the youth pastor's title. And of course, when
the website goes down or becomes outdated, many youth pastors find
themselves becoming the church's unofficial technology director/repair
person.

If a church is fortunate enough to have a youth ministry whose size
justifies a full-time youth pastor's salary, the "successful" youth worker
almost always winds up trading time with teenagers for time planning
and promoting events and programs. As a result, in many exemplar
youth ministries, the people most gifted and equipped to spend time

cultivating relationships and lifelong faith in young people often become the least available to them.

3. Training Realities

I have begun to wonder if most of our training for youth ministry is unintentionally designed for those who need it least. Here's what I mean:

My colleague Stephanie Caro is one of the country's foremost experts on small church ministry. She reminds me frequently that the average size church in America is only seventy-six people and that the average size youth group is eight.[43] A 2018 study echoes Stephanie's claim enough to give us pause:

> Two simple statistics help explain the American church. There are other important church stats, but these two may surprise you.
>
> 1. The median church size is 75 people.
> 2. The median church age is 73 years.[44]

Yet the primary focus of youth ministry training has been directed toward those trying to build full-blown youth *programs,* with attractional events, trips, multiple weekly gatherings, etc. All the while, there seems to be little to no cultivation of those responsible for leading Jesus-sized youth groups of twelve or so. These leaders of mini youth groups typically don't have the time or money or exposure to attend trainings, read books, or deepen their competency in youth ministry.

Do a search for "volunteer youth workers," and you'll find that almost everything is designed to help "professional" youth workers recruit and train *their* volunteers. But almost no resources are available to help the ten-hours-a-week (or less) youth worker thrive—much less the five-hour-a-week volunteer youth pastor.

Of course, it all makes sense. The very part-time volunteer youth worker is often recruited by their desperate pastor to serve for "just a year." Once they begin, they are (often unintentionally) expected to "compete" with program-based youth ministries and to offer fellowship, mission, and family events.

These kinds of youth workers don't yet exist as a tribe, making it next to impossible to gather them as a group. And yet when I think of them, there is something in the back of my mind, and a stirring in my gut, that makes me believe we are missing an opportunity whose time has come.

4. Emotional Realities

Most full-time youth workers I know (and I know quite a few) feel exhausted, misunderstood, pressured to produce, and more than a little guilty about how little time they are giving their family, their health, and their own spiritual vitality. Most are running at a pace that virtually guarantees that they will not be doing youth ministry far beyond the time when they actually figure out what they are doing.

I did youth ministry for fourteen years full-time at one church, and then continued to manage the ministry from a part-time position for fourteen more years. Ultimately, it was the exhaustion that got me. I've never before put this in print, but I just couldn't imagine doing one more trip. As much as I wanted to, as crucial as I believed the work was, at fifty-six years old, I just couldn't.

The further I get from my own work as a "professional" youth worker and the more I observe the next generation of youth workers, the less surprised I am that so few stay in this field for more than a few years.

As I write this, we are moving (we hope) to the final months of the 2020 pandemic—a pandemic that has exacerbated the exhaustion of many pastors. A recent Barna study reported that in 2016, 14% of pastors said their mental and emotional health was average to poor. By April 2020, that number more than doubled, growing to 35%. In August 2020, fully 50% of pastors said their mental and emotional health was average to poor.[45]

Many pastors are finding themselves targets of increased criticism, while seeing their workload multiply dramatically. Thom Rainer has observed the growing prevalence of this pattern:

> The vast majority of pastors with whom our team communicates are saying they are considering quitting their churches. It's a trend I

have not seen in my lifetime.[46]

David Kinnaman echoed this sentiment in a recent tweet: "I've never seen data like this in my 25 years of research. The resilience of pastors is being tested like no other time in our lives."[47]

When the pandemic and post-pandemic realities are added to the already perfect storm of other factors, we can predict that the pressure on youth workers will only increase over the next couple of decades. It will become even more normal for supervisors and well-meaning stakeholders to question why their youth worker just can't achieve the results the church saw decades ago.

The long hours, low pay, and unrealistic expectations make me wonder why I never stopped to question whether our current model is good, healthy, or effective. It's all enough to make me question whether the standard model of full-time, professional youth worker actually has a future.

Some have suggested that we are witnessing the end of youth ministry. I don't think so. I think we may be seeing an end to a model of youth ministry that has proven to be short-sighted and problematic on many levels.

And like I said, this shift might not be such a bad thing.

Imagining the New Future

Established churches, like established businesses, are not famous for their willingness to innovate. The story of the fall of Kodak has become an almost cliché cautionary tale of the dangers at getting better and better at delivering what people are going to need less and less. The once unparalleled name in photography *and the early inventor of digital photography*, Kodak went bankrupt in 2012, with many pointing to Kodak's "safe" decision to double down on their historic strength— film—rather than investing in the unproven innovation of digital photography.

Most churches—especially established churches—steadfastly cling to strategies that may have worked quite effectively thirty, forty, or fifty years earlier. Most are doubling down, trying to do better at what they have already done in the past.

The future of youth ministry depends on how churches respond to a single fundamental question: Will we seek to be better and better prepared for a world that no longer exists, or will we pivot into the unknown, the experimental, the uncertain?

We may not be able to predict the future of youth ministry, but I can identify at least a few seismic shifts will almost certainly take place in the next twenty to thirty years:

1. Fewer and fewer churches will be able to afford full-time youth workers, and many churches will transition to volunteer-led ministries (a reality that few people seem to want to pay attention to).

2. We can also expect that effective, engaging, faithful youth ministry will still require just as many resources as it has in the past, likely more.

3. Churches that cannot imagine faithful ministry to teenagers without a paid youth worker are in for a crash.

4. The ministries that survive will find creative means of funding ministry far beyond what can reasonably be expected using anticipated funding streams.

5. Many who have trained for a vocation in church-based youth ministry will find it increasingly difficult to find a full-time position, and many who remain in vocational youth ministry will likely need to find additional sources of revenue to support themselves.

Though to some these predictions might sound grim, I happen to believe that youth ministry's best days are ahead of us.

While it's far from guaranteed, I am hopeful that the church's current desperation will inspire unprecedented creativity. Before I share a few modest proposals for the future of youth ministry, I want to offer a few aspirational snapshots of what youth ministry might be, and could be, if we are intentional about crafting the future while there is still time:

1. The varied expressions of youth ministry—church and parachurch, tribal and multicultural, denominational and non-denominational, national and global—have the chance to come together with a unified vision on behalf of the next generation. Our friends at the Fuller Youth Institute have, over the past decade, made huge strides in mapping and connecting youth ministry influencers from a wide theological and institutional spectrum.

2. We can widen our lens to understand youth ministry beyond the limited horizon built into an approach that disproportionately invests in youth ministry for white, suburban contexts.

3. We have the chance to expand the focus of youth ministry to include those who are traditionally excluded from typical youth ministry approaches, including immigrant youth, special needs youth, and others whom the church has historically marginalized.

4. Given the anticipated financial cliff facing the church, we can find creative ways to fund youth ministries and youth ministers.

5. Those with a calling and gifts for youth ministry might stay in the game much longer if they could work more directly with fewer teenagers, rather than spending the majority of their time keeping programmatic machines running.

6. The assumption that youth ministry belongs only to the professionally-trained, full-time youth worker can become a thing of the past, opening the door to thousands who are gifted for youth ministry but have not chosen the role of a paid, professional youth worker.

7. Youth ministry of the future can create a platform for youth agency in which young people design, invent, test, and reinvent missional enterprises aligned with the gospel.

I will leave it to others (including perhaps other authors of this book) to address the first three dreams I have outlined above. In this chapter, I will focus my attention on the immense possibilities inherent in the impending shifts

- from full-time youth workers to very part-time and volunteer youth workers

- from church-dependent funding to creatively-sourced funding of youth ministers and youth ministries
- From youth as spectators and consumers to youth as agents of ministry themselves

There is still time, if we are willing to begin the pivot now.

A Few Modest Proposals

It is clear that the need for youth ministry in the coming decades will be as great as it ever has been. It is also clear that this work can no longer depend on the standard delivery system of full-time youth pastors and traditional youth groups.

What is unclear is what new delivery systems, out of many unfolding new approaches, might become the new standard or standards. Though much is uncertain, I can identify three budding expressions of youth ministry that may hold at least some of the seeds of the future of youth ministry.

Economic Alternatives:
Youth Pastor as Missional Entrepreneur

In our work with Ministry Incubators,[48] we have been inspired, again and again, by wildly creative approaches to the funding and the practice of ministry. I'll share just three examples of experimental initiatives that have found ways to practice youth ministry as a social enterprise. The magic of these ministries is that their economic engines are not just the way they *fund* ministry; the enterprises themselves actually *are* the place where ministry takes place. Though each is unique in its approach, all three use the employment of teenagers as a platform for discipleship.

Try Pie,[49] launched and led by the wildly creative power duo of Megan Tensen and Sarah Helleso. This ministry grew out of a creative partnership between two radically missional churches from two radically different contexts, one in Cedar Falls, Iowa, and the other in nearby Waterloo.

Try Pie employs young women, making and selling pies, as a platform for engaging and equipping them for their futures. Each young person on the Try Pie team has a mentor and is surrounded by a nurturing community of peers and adults who together shape the teenagers' faith, confidence, and job readiness.

All student employees "learn to manage their paychecks, prepare for future employment, understand their unique gifts, and recognize value in each other." Over the past few years, Try Pie has experienced significant growth, now with its own storefront and food truck. Sarah says, "There's so much missed if we try to piece out what's 'sacred' and 'secular.' There is an overlap between business and ministry, and God is in it."[50]

MowTown Teen Lawn Care*[51] *was dreamed up by Matt Overton when he was the Associate Pastor for Youth and Their Families at Columbia Presbyterian Church in Vancouver, Washington. As Matt explained, "In youth ministry, we attract kids all the time with Cheetos, couches, and games. Why not attract them with jobs and work and life skills?"[52]

Since the launch of MowTown, Matt and his enterprise, Columbia Future Forge,[53] have expanded their focus beyond just youth employment through creative partnerships that align gospel-centered ethics with human transformation. Now at 125 students strong, this work currently includes a drone pilot certification program (Forge Drone Piloting), Utmost Athletics (an affordable, sliding scale strength training program), and partnerships with multiple high schools.

It is no surprise that Matt is quickly becoming a leading voice in conversations related to innovative, entrepreneurial approaches to youth ministry. He is not only personally doing the-future-is-now ministry but also training adults to do ministry outside of the narrowly defined approaches of traditional youth programs. Through it all, the program is designed around robust theological reflection, asking the question, "What does the way we are doing ministry actually reveal about what we believe about God?"[54]

Go Fish*[55] *was launched by Matt McNelly, head of staff at a church in the Pacific Northwest who found himself in the unenviable position of the church needing to cut his salary to make budget. Around the same time, Matt also read that the "dam people" (that is, the Bonneville

Power Administration) were offering $5-$8 a fish for anyone catching pikeminnows, a predatory fish responsible for the loss of millions of salmon fingerlings every year on the Snake and Columbia River systems.

At first Matt thought of this possibility as a straightforward tentmaking opportunity. But the more he considered it, the more he realized its massive ministry potential. Go Fish now offers youth, age ten and older, the chance to "Save Salmon. Explore Creation. Earn Money. Encounter Christ." In the spirit of Someone else who combined discipleship and fishing, the Go Fish experience is described as "a floating monastic community, with days on the boat ordered with times of prayer, sacred readings, periods of silence, shared meals, and discussions of faith."[56]

The beauty of all three of these ministries is that the number of hours youth spend working in these enterprises alongside godly adults is exponentially greater than those youth would have ever experienced by faithfully attending traditional youth programs every week. And all of them provide both funding for ministry and income for the young people participating. Win. Win. And (discipleship) Win.

Small Wins:
100,000 Hernia-Free Very Part-Time Youth Workers
When it comes to cultivating lifelong disciples, small wins. It worked for Jesus, and if we're honest, most of us have had our own faith shaped most profoundly in a circle of fewer than twenty companions, usually fewer than twelve.

As I think back on my own discipleship journey as a teenager, it is clear that being part of a big crowd of peers gathering regularly (the holy grail of so many churches' understanding of youth ministry, and what most churches specifically hire a youth worker to accomplish) was not what made the difference. What made the difference for me, and I'll bet what made the difference for most Christian adults, were the small things that happened in small ways with a small group of people. Small wins.

Given the anticipated fragility of the institution of professional youth ministry (see the financial realities, emotional realities, training realities, and impact realities listed above), I want to dream a not-so-modest dream.

What if what the church (and the world) needs at this pivotal moment in our history is not more professional, full-time youth workers but 100,000 or so hernia-free volunteers who are each actively engaged with a handful of young people, week in and week out? Kara Powell and the good folks at the Fuller Youth Institute have a dream of bringing 100,000 churches more intentionally into the process of discipling young people. Why not make the focus of those 100,000 churches (or a good portion of them) small churches that can't afford a full-time (and maybe can't afford even a part-time) paid youth worker?

What if we could shift our primary youth ministry training focus from the professionals in youth ministry to the volunteer (or nearly volunteer) youth ministers? What if we could create an ecology of support that engaged, connected, equipped, and inspired this group on the front line of youth ministry? What if this ecosystem could set free the immense gifts of people like Rick Lawrence to lead kids as highly skilled amateurs—from the French *amateur*, from Latin *amātōrem* ("lover"), from amāre ("to love")[57]—not as a part of a job upon which their livelihood depends?

Over my twenty-eight years at First Presbyterian in Nashville, I had the privilege of working with around a couple dozen wildly gifted young adults who, for a season, worked full-time on our youth staff. I could tell you about Scott and Jacquie and Brandon and Erika and Teddy and Courtney and Josh and Margaret Ann and Adam N and Adam D and Millie and Matt and BJ and Leigh and Trey and Ginger and Jay and Colyer and Debbie and Kirk and Mark.

Quite a few are still in ministry of one kind or another—some are pastors, a couple are professors, one is a musician, a few work in nonprofits. All still love Jesus. But only four are currently serving in any form of vocational youth ministry. And apart from those who get paid for it, only a very few of them are investing intentionally in the lives of teenagers at all.

What if those of us who have been a part of the Youth Ministry Industrial Complex started with a focus on those who *used to* do youth ministry, those who, for whatever reason (and there are plenty!) couldn't see themselves working with teenagers for a living? What if we asked them to minister to youth—but we didn't ask them to organize events or update Facebook or write newsletter articles or plan trips or recruit an endless slew of volunteers?

We could take away the weight of self-criticism that comes with being compared to the megachurch down the street. There would be no committee approval necessary for changing the schedule, the approach, the methodology. We would simply invite them to make space for an hour or so a week for teenagers whom God might bring into their lives. Instead of doing trips for kids and with kids, these leaders could send them off in pairs or small groups to experience incredible ministry all over the country—*planned by someone else!*[58]

I am making the audacious suggestion that one can be a highly effective youth pastor in five to ten hours a week. When we take away the counterproductive demand to gather a large group of young people to church meetings, these volunteer or nearly volunteer youth workers get to do what they love—actually work with teenagers—with little to no concern about how many kids show up.

Could we blur the line between professional and volunteer youth workers, with very few youth workers depending on the church for the money they need to live on? Yes, I'm suggesting that the best youth workers are those who have a life and an identity outside of youth ministry.

To sum up: What if we shifted our focus from training the leaders of big youth ministries to cultivating 100,000 hernia-free, very part-time youth workers, ordinarily investing far fewer than ten hours a week in fewer than ten youth at a time? What if we started by simply asking people to be open to God using them to gather and support a group of young people and listening to, praying with, and supporting them in their spiritual lives? I might suggest these simple commitments:

1. Would you pray regularly for the teenagers who are already in your life?

2. Would you ask God for eyes to see the teenagers in your community who are longing for a small circle of friends in faith?

3. Could you create space in your heart and schedule to meet regularly with a group of ten or so teenagers, should God bring them to you?

4. Will you find a friend in faith (or several) with whom you could pray and work together on this project?

And what if we created a bank of resources tailor-made for adults willing to work together to create intentional space for youth to be heard, to be taken seriously, and to be invited into the delightful and perplexing unpredictability of following Jesus?

Instead of continuing to pour all our training, development, and equipping energy into youth workers who have a continuing ed budget, what if we created a national, cross-pollinated, rotating network of youth worker cohorts that gathered, like AA groups, on a regular basis to ensure a healthy ecosystem for tending to the next generation?

What if the Lilly Endowment would fund the first iteration for the first 1,000 folks?

What if the Templeton Foundation would fund the next iteration for 50,000 folks?

What if the old goat youth pastors like Rick and Marko and Doug and me (I would never call Kara, Kenda, and Jeanne goats or old, but I would want them in the conversation) worked to build out the framework of a worldwide garden in which this kind of ecosystem could thrive? Even the possibility of getting an army of youth ministry mad scientists, like Rick Lawrence, out there doing ministry in their basements, backyards, and on Zoom makes it well worth the investment.

And Yet:
Youth Pastor as Platform Creator and Laboratory Manager

Even thirty years from now there will continue to be churches that will prioritize having a full-time youth pastor. These churches will have a choice. They can keep trying harder to do the traditional models of youth ministry better, treating youth primarily as spectators of adult leaders' faith and expertise. Or they can become laboratories for the future of youth ministry and provide platforms for youth to serve as agents of ministry, rather than consumers of it.

The Changemaker Initiative[59] at Los Altos United Methodist Church in Los Altos, California, is seeking to do youth ministry in just this way. Both the youth ministry and the children's ministry are leaning in to the church's fundamental changemaker DNA, built on the assumption that the best discipleship happens when we are joining in the changemaking work that God is already doing in the world.

Instead of spending so much time trying to get young people to attend our meetings and buy into our visions, we can create space to go to *their* meetings and buy into *their* visions. What if it were normal for sixteen-, seventeen-, and eighteen-year-old young people to serve as ministry interns, rather than bored consumers of the same menu of programs they have had since they were twelve?

Make no mistake about it. This approach to youth ministry will be much slower than the paint-by-numbers approach of youth group, small groups, and mission trips. And though the standard components of youth ministry will likely still be necessary in some form, in this new approach, they'll become a platform for youth discerning and delivering ministry themselves.

Youth might dream up a youth ministry version of Teach for America. They might develop a cooking ministry that provides homemade meals to first responders or people at risk. They might design a worship technology toolkit for smaller churches to use to expand the impact of their online worship experience. Or they might create a safe space for immigrants or friends who are struggling with isolation, loneliness, and depression. In Ministry Incubator's hatchathons,[60] we have had the joy of seeing so many of these dreams begin to blossom and grow when young people are given the space and the environment to create and to be taken seriously as partners in ministry.

Making It Personal

I left my paid youth ministry position in 2014. I had been a youth pastor for over thirty-five years. Youth ministry is the one thing I know best. I might even say that it is the thing I was made for.

Yet I'm realizing (insert facepalm emoji) that the only framework I have had for doing youth ministry myself was as a staff person, paid to work with young people. When I retired from the church, I involuntarily assumed that my youth ministry days were over.

As I moved on to other ministry projects, I simply didn't have the imagination to see that I didn't need to leave youth ministry behind. I could take a page from my favorite youth ministry mad scientist and create space for a handful of youth to cocreate ministry.

I'm realizing too that there is a handful teenagers right now who I know and love at the tiny churches where I currently serve, and I'm embarrassed to say that I have done next to nothing to create space for them. Just because I don't have time to create a busy calendar of programming doesn't mean I can't create space to give them attention.

We have the chance to cultivate a fundamentally different ecology surrounding youth ministry, not one built on the assumption of "professional" youth workers. I spent much of my life investing in and promoting the expansion of the profession of youth ministry, believing that there is no more important work for the church of Jesus Christ than youth ministry, that nothing matters quite like the work of creating space for young people to know and live into God's delight in them.

I still believe that.

The mission and its priority haven't changed, but the delivery system must. May God give us grace to sing a new song.

HOW I'M DOING THIS

SARAH HELLESO

When I read Mark's chapter, I was instantly thrilled for future readers. Wisdom, my friends. That's what just came at you. A little anecdotal sidebar might help at this point to give a concrete example of what this new future of youth ministry might look like—at least in our slice of Iowa.

Try Pie is very different from the pizza parties and lock-ins I grew up with. (For starters, we make and sell dessert pies, not pizza pies.) Though I'm still very much behind pizza parties, I'm drawn to how the social enterprise model, which integrates so much of what's been kept separate, shows where God is at work. In our experience with Try Pie, the social enterprise model has started to move us toward the holy repair of what's been pulled apart. And maybe this holy repair can start, as lots of good things do, with the youngest leaders.

Try Pie's storefront is in Waterloo, one of the two towns that make up Iowa's Cedar Valley. Its affluent college-town counterpart, Cedar Falls, gives stark contrast to Waterloo's historically racially and socioeconomically diverse demographic. The murders of Ahmaud Arbery, George Floyd, and Breonna Taylor in the first half of 2020 brought attention once again to the deep wounds of injustice our communities continue to work to lament, address, and heal. For many youth and young adults, a realization of the church's complicity, if not participation, in a list of offenses comes soon after events like these. We can't ignore this. The next generation is asking us to engage these issues, and, maybe, that ask could help us notice where God is inviting the church to move next in learning to love our neighbors.

Try Pie purposefully hires a diverse group of teens from high schools in both Waterloo and Cedar Falls, offering jobs to meet a common need among uncommon friends. Most of our teenagers admit to being unlikely to befriend or even cross paths with teammates at Try Pie if they didn't work in the kitchen together. God created us to experience and advocate for the kind of diversity that allows us to see all of humanity as being made in his image. We miss out on that—and I would suggest, diminish that truth—when our ministries catch a limited portion of the kingdom. We have to think differently, and be humbly intentional, about understanding the divides in our communities to move into a different future.

Starting a business is one way to step into that new space for ministry. A business has to interact with its community and will either contribute to or detract from that community's overall well-being. In this context, a business can naturally become an example of the proximity and presence with which Jesus approached the world to communicate the truest thing about it: We are all loved children of God, made with great purpose. Try Pie teens close each shift by speaking a version of these words as an affirmation to each other, and they revisit that truth throughout their work. With space for each teenager to use her gifts, see the gifts of her peers, and contribute to the work of Try Pie, something as simple as rolling out pie crust becomes a holy moment, a vibrant opportunity to experience who they are and who God is.

As Mark nodded to in this chapter, a social enterprise can give youth a chance to not only participate in, but to lead in and create the ministry they are part of. In Try Pie, each teen serves on a business development committee that takes charge of everything including recipe development, finance, marketing, and running our summer food truck. This illustrates the important point that if we're willing to see it, work could actually be a way for us to holistically care for teens, and to help them recognize their ability to join in the reconciling work God is doing in any space where they find themselves.

With the right mix of prayer, relationships, market research, and partnership, starting a social enterprise-structured youth ministry can be financially reasonable. YES! When your "business" has a basic product that also serves as a tool to achieve ministry goals, youth experience and revenue can support each other and create something sustainable. As Try Pie grew and it made sense to become our own 501(c)3 nonprofit (the reasoning here could be a whole other book), the church we are affiliated with generously maintained staffing costs.

Support from the church and a strong revenue stream can change the financial game in volatile times. Despite the many challenges of 2020, during that year 80% of the remaining expenses to run the program (beyond those staff salaries the church paid) were covered by pie sales. This unique partnership comes with a grace-required learning curve. But by stretching the muscles of creativity and teamwork, it has the potential to bring about major impact, the kind we'll strive to repeat. A product-based revenue stream invites connection with people who may never walk into, let alone give to, a church. Here in this middle ground of social enterprise ministry, we can connect with people who can catch a glimpse of the hope we have as they make a purchase and support this work.

Creating a business/ministry combination program might feel like uncharted territory, but in this possibility I think you'll find there's a peace that's sourced from aligning with the wholeness God created us for.

Church and community. Work and faith. Growing pains and freedom to grow. Diversity embraced. Boldness balanced with humility. Though the model breaks with tradition, so much of it feels good and right and whole. Joy and peace to you, friends.

Sarah Helleso directs the Try Pie Bakery program alongside her codirector, Megan Tensen. Sarah studied business and nonprofit management while attending the University of Northern Iowa before moving to the east side of Waterloo, Iowa. Living and working alongside the students she serves in a community she loves is a gift she's grateful for.

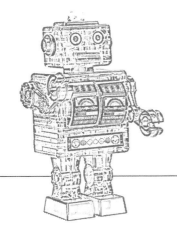

VIEW 4:
ENGAGING **ALL**
FAMILIES

BY VIRGINIA WARD

Engaging all families in the church sounds like a daunting task for any youth worker. The process of attracting, influencing, and engaging families has become more than a full-time job for one person, and is even challenging for many teams. There are always new youth and families coming into our ministries who ultimately join the pool of existing families. Regardless of your years of service in youth ministry, as this continues to happen the old tried and proven connection points may no longer apply. The simple truth is that our homogenous church environments are unable to effectively minister to every family. As we look to the future, the way we approach ministering to all families is critically important.

Before we go any further, I think it is important to define a couple of terms. First, the phrase "all families" simply means all families with teenagers who have attended any of the worship services, youth group, big events, camps, etc. that are held by a church. For these families, there was a defined initial connection point either through a parent, youth leader, or youth attending the church. We must also include those who have made digital connections, as with the increased use of technology and social media, youth and families are discovering churches without a prior personal connection. It's important to note that there is a broad scope falling under the definition of "all families," with all types of people groups from varied walks of life expecting spiritual support from our churches. Anyone working in youth ministry is challenged to expand their hospitality to include new people who may not have any idea of their church's culture or expectations.

The next term, "engagement," can be described as the level to which a family takes part in the programs or services of the ministry. Engagement is difficult to predict because each family will choose what level of engagement they desire. And going a step further, decisions about church involvement are determined through the lens of each family member. Once the church has touched the family in any way, the pursuit of a long-term relationship with any or all of the family members must be mutual and reciprocal.

The evolution of the family composition over the years presents an interesting challenge to the church. The initial findings of the 2020 United States Census confirm the changing demographics of the American family, particularly America's racial demography.[61] William Frey addresses this diversity explosion and its impact on generational change, regional shifts of major racial groups, neighborhood segregation, and interracial marriage.[62] This generational divide in diversity—named a "cultural generation gap" by Frey—has serious implications on the composition of the families in our churches and youth ministries. Because of the changing ethnic landscape of our country, communities are becoming more diverse. The old school of thought that the white, middle-class standard is the only way of ministry does not hold true. Diversity is changing the way we do things. Youth in the US now represent the country's most diverse generation. This changing ethnic landscape of the church ushers in an opportunity for families to engage—if the church extends its arms to all families. Churches who do the homework now and prepare to receive all families will be ready to embrace all ethnic communities.

The classic 1967 American movie *Guess Who's Coming to Dinner* follows the journey of an interracial couple and their families. As the plot unfolds, this movie provides a few lessons for the church to consider when it comes to cultural generation gaps:

- Neither family was prepared for who arrived on their doorstep.
- Neither family wanted to engage with the other, regardless of a newly-formed relationship.
- Neither family knew quite what to do.
- Both families had to make a few adjustments in the name of love.
- The younger members of each family required the older members of the families to change.

This may feel quite familiar to you given our present circumstances, when we are recovering from a pandemic and are in the midst of addressing, and often failing to address, issues of health and race. I think this all comes together to create a *selah* moment, a chance for us to pause and reflect. So let's pause, and reflect on what it really means for our ministries to engage all families.

My personal theology of youth ministry requires family engagement. I believe the church is the place where families are strengthened, equipped, healed, and restored. Youth ministry without the family is a travesty. Because of these beliefs, my church and youth leadership teams established a framework to engage all families early in the relationship-building process, regardless of any family's ethnic, economic, or social composition. Some families have responded and connected with the church, while others choose to remain distant. Regardless of where a family landed on our engagement spectrum, we were intentional about our communication.

According to Reggie Joiner of Orange, the ultimate strategy of engagement is for leaders to

> influence those who
> influence those who
> influence the next generation.[63]

In other words, if the church will prepare itself to engage all families, there will be greater influence with the next generation.

This chapter will raise various challenges that need to be addressed by the church in order for youth ministries to effectively engage all families. My prayer is for you to read this information with an open mind and heart. Allow God to address the areas of your ministry that need adjusting to include all families.

A Broader View of Family

When people use the word "family," the image that comes to mind often includes a two-parent or a single-parent household where everyone is related. The definition of family according to *Merriam-Webster* refers to a group of persons with common ancestry living under one roof and usually under one head. *Merriam-Webster* also states that a family is the basic unit of society, having as its nucleus two adults, a father and mother living together and cooperating in the care and rearing of their own or adopted children.[64]

Many sociologists are in debate regarding the definition of family. Some suggest the bedrock of the family is a marriage between a man and a woman. Society has traditionally held this view as sacred and exclusive. Many agree that the first lessons in life are learned inside the walls of the home. The family is the base where work, care, service, healing, and worship are common elements,[65] and the start of life is with a family.

Many other sociologists, though, contend that the new definition of family can be inclusive of genetic and legal bonds, but not limited to either. Broadly defined, in this view family consists of a recognized group of individuals who form an emotional connection and serves as an economic unit of society.[66] Even the US Census counts people living together as a part of the household or family, whether or not there is a blood relation.

To expand on this second view, a more current definition of family is one that provides its members with emotional and spiritual kinship through:

- Shared values, beliefs, and traditions
- Common experiences and activities
- Unconditional, non-judgmental support[67]

The evolution of the family must be considered as ministries prepare to engage all families. Pew Research Center, for instance, determined that there is no longer one dominant family form in the United States.[68] There are multiple types of family structures. The following list is a starting point to consider:

- Traditional nuclear family—mother, father, children of a suburban, middle-class family
- Traditional mother, father, children in a lower socioeconomic family
- Adopted/foster families
- Single parents
- Never-married families
- Blended families (16% of US families[69])
- Ethnic-specific families
- Multiethnic families by marriage or adoption
- Single parent families living in a larger, extended family where aunts and uncles, other generations, etc. live and work toward shared goals (common with immigrant families)
- Families for whom English is not the first language
- Childless families—couples who cannot or choose not to have children
- Grandparent families (one in four children is being raised by a grandparent; in some ethnic communities an official adoption may not actually take place through the courts)
- Families with children who have special needs
- Same-gender parent families
- Surrogate parent families
- Families with sperm donors who choose to not be identified, and those with sperm donors who are identified

Truth be told, parts of this expanded definition of the family existed in Bible times. The first surrogate, ethnically-mixed family originated with Abraham, Sarah, and Hagar. And while the social definition of family has changed, the biblical definition of family has not. There are two major streams of family noted in the Scriptures: those connected by blood and those who are adopted into the family. Both streams provide a resting place for family members. Psalm 68:6 states that God sets the lonely in families, which shows the intentionality of God to use the family unit as a connecting point for all individuals.

Historically, though, the church has interpreted the biblical view of family through a social lens that does not represent all families. The current youth ministry format was designed to support families from one defined and accepted structure: a two-parent, middle-class, ethnic-specific home consisting of a related father, mother, and children. Ministries in American-based youth ministry assume the standard family is middle-class, white, and suburban, with characteristics like two-parent homes, mothers attending PTA meetings, kids driving cars in high school, and college-bound students. The expectation that families have summer vacations shapes program models. Middle-class ethnic Americans who have crossed the economic divide have bought into this model, often disregarding their ethnic traditions.

Youth ministry in churches that do not comply with the traditionally accepted family structure have adapted the known models and discovered alternative ways to minister to families.

As we look to engage all families, it's critical that we be aware of the issues that affect all families. Educators, doctors, and other professionals who connect with families on a regular basis have identified a basic list of challenges that affect families, regardless of their socioeconomic standing. Of these, we must look especially closely at economics, environmental pressures, cultural intelligence, and trauma.

1. Economics in Play

In *Our America*, LeAlan Jones and Lloyd Newman boldly outline a reality different from the middle-class norm described above for many families in America.[70] The differences in resources for certain ethnic communities greatly affects how ministry to families occurs. Ethnic urban and rural families in lower-income brackets traverse through life in a different manner than families in other income brackets. Homes with mortgages are replaced with rentals. Cars for teens are replaced with public transportation and bicycles. Mothers working in the home are replaced with working mothers. Savings accounts are rare to nonexistent. Single families living in one home are replaced with multiple intergenerational families living in one apartment.

The financial health of a family is a major stressor for families of all ethnicities. Families living in poverty face additional stressors such as financial hardships, residential instability, food insecurities, and discrimination. As quiet as this truth is kept, your zip code matters. City families are a mix of mostly blue-collar workers who make their income from service industry and manual labor types of jobs. There are also some white-collar families whose members make their income from desk jobs that require them to wear suits. Zip codes for suburban families are generally made up of white-collar workers with a smaller number of blue-collar workers. Middle-class families in the city tend to be a combination of mostly renters and some homeowners. While gentrification has affected the economic make-up of the city, the economic inequities persist.

Looking through the lenses of resources and money, it's clear that middle-class city life is different from middle-class suburban life. The Federal Reserve Bank of Boston collected data in a report entitled "The Color of Wealth in Boston," in which they analyzed the debt and assets of families in the greater Boston area. In the analysis, they reviewed debt and asset estimates for US-born Blacks, Caribbean Blacks, Cape Verdeans, Puerto Ricans, and Dominicans in the Boston Metropolitan Statistical Area (MSA). The data collected on white households and nonwhite households exhibited large differences. The net worth of whites and that of nonwhites is staggeringly divergent.[71]

A key finding of the report is that nonwhite households have only a fraction of the net worth attributed to white households. While white households have a median wealth of $247,500, Dominicans and US Blacks have a median wealth of close to zero. Of all nonwhite groups for which estimates could be made, Caribbean Black households have the highest median wealth with $12,000, which is only 5% of the wealth attributed to white households in the Boston MSA (See Exhibit A).[72]

City, state, and federal resources are allocated differently depending on the demographic area in which families reside. The exposure to new and expanded experiences as well as resources sets the values and goals of youth and their families. The socioeconomic standing of a family grants increased access to resources and connections. In other words, your zip code is enormously important.

Respected educator Jawanza Kunjufu believes that Black youth must be motivated and prepared to succeed financially in order to break the economic cycles that have kept so many families in poverty.[73]

Wealth in Boston Report
Exhibit A[74]. Chart reprinted thanks to permission from the Federal Reserve Bank of Boston.

While all families face challenges economically, they manifest differently depending on the family's income bracket. While one family faces a decision of what type of car to purchase and where to purchase that car, another family rejoices over the school-provided bus pass for their children and negotiates the cost of a bus pass for each parent.

2. Environmental Challenges—From the City to the Suburbs

Most of the cities in the ancient Near East had a specified role as a fortified guardian for the families living within their gates and the natural resources within. Cities in the Old Testament were also known as places of refuge (Numbers 26:55; Joshua 14:2; 1 Samuel 14:41-42). Some cities reflected their commitment to God, while others were built in rebellion. In the New Testament, we see that Jesus's ministry served both the countryside and the city. His prayers for Jerusalem not only referred to a people group but to the geographical region:

a city. Jerusalem would become the place of resurrection, ascension, and Pentecost, and serve as the starting point for all apostolic mission ventures.[75] While civilization started in a garden, it will find resolution in a city.

The city has a different sound. The pace of the city is faster, the sounds of the city are louder, and the heart of the city is open to receiving people and institutions of all kinds. In the city, constant movement through traffic, music, and the diversity of people are normative. City families are watchful, protective, persistent, and direct—in other words, they have grit. Youth and adults in cities develop a tenacity that will not allow them to quit, even in dire circumstances.

Families nurtured in the city have learned over time to adjust quickly to an ever-changing landscape. Adaptability is a necessary skill that is sharpened through various mental and physical exercises. The suburbs are not as fast-moving, which can contribute to youth and their families developing a naive mindset. Often suburban parents will warn their young ones to be on guard in the city, but don't know what exactly to tell them to look out for. It's also true that some suburban youth find the city to be exciting, welcoming the challenges of the pace.

The city is the measuring rod for the suburbs. Cultural trends begin in cities globally and are eventually reflected in the surrounding towns. In a similar way, the city can be the measuring rod for family ministry. Family ministry in the city displays inclusive, bible-based engagement that can be helpful for the suburbs.

3. Ethnic and Cultural Intelligence

Over time, many changes have occurred to the ethnic and cultural landscape of America. It is important for youth ministry leaders to factor these changes into their planning.

> The U.S. today is a melting pot of cultures, thanks to increasing ethnic and racial diversification. If the trend continues, America will be more colorful than ever by 2045, at which point no single ethnic group will constitute the majority in the U.S. for the first time. But with immigration reform still a hot-button issue, the U.S. ethnic landscape may change again in the near future.[76]

David Livermore, a social scientist who leads the Cultural Intelligence Center in Lansing, Michigan, defines cultural intelligence (CQ) as

> the capability to function effectively across a variety of cultural contexts, such as ethnic, generational, and organizational cultures. CQ has some similarities with various approaches to cultural competence but it differs in its specific ties to intelligence research. As a result, the emphasis is not only on understanding different cultures, but also on problem solving and effective adaptions for various cultural settings.[77]

Livermore further states that the CQ model acknowledges that our multicultural interactions are also personal, individualized experiences. The same ethnic background may not yield the same cross-cultural experience. For example, an Asian-American who grew up in a predominantly white context may not identify with the first-generation Asian-American who grew up in an Asian-specific context. While they might share the same ethnic heritage, their experiences within their specific settings might be drastically different.

Technology has plunged youth into a globally interconnected experience as a daily reality. Youth are engaging in more cross-cultural relationships than their parents and, sadly often, their youth leaders. Youth are connecting in digital spaces with others outside of their tribes—but some of our churches are not reflecting that diversity.

Neighborhoods in the city serve as melting pots for African-American, Latinx, Asian-American, and white families, as well as other ethnicities. City families celebrate diversity in subtle ways by sharing knowledge and honoring differences. Similarities can be found between families despite language and ethnic variances. Culture competence, or the ability to understand your own culture and respectfully interact with other cultures, is an aspect of the social competencies necessary for human development. The Search Institute lists culture competence as an internal asset for young people.[78]

In some immigrant communities, ethnic customs are questioned and abandoned by younger generations who want to identify with the American culture they were raised in since birth. Older, non-English-speaking, first-generation adults often long for the benefits of America without compromising their childhood and cultural experiences. This can cause a clash in the generations.

For urban youth and families, cross-cultural training takes place in real time. Through common childhood games played by all of the youth in the neighborhood such as hide and seek, jump rope, and jacks, children learn that everybody who speaks with a Caribbean accent was not born in Jamaica. The annual Caribbean Festival held in a local park of various cities can serve as the learning lab for the community. The sounds and smells of various Caribbean countries self-instruct youth how to distinguish someone from Jamaica, or from Haiti, or from Barbados, or from Cape Verde.

Youth also learn that everybody who speaks with a Spanish accent is not Puerto Rican. Dominican and other Latinx community members introduce the community to another world right on their front porches. By the time youth in the city enter high school, their ethnic intelligence is extremely high.

Lack of diversity in some environments positions youth for low cultural intelligence and aids in perpetuating the ills of society. Lessons learned from the city can provide a great framework for suburban churches desiring to increase diversity. As gentrification and urban sprawl increase, the diversity in traditionally homogeneous suburban spaces will require churches to make some adjustments.

4. Trauma

Trauma has become a norm for most families, regardless of their income status. Violence has visited families in new ways via the internet, and mass shootings at schools and other venues have reduced the sense of safety with youth and children. Trauma-based mental health issues are on the rise in youth and their families. Stress-based and anxiety-based disorders now rank high on the list, along with depression and suicide.[79] The dark side of the world of children and teens is more visible than ever before. Increased rates of stress revealing themselves through depression and suicide in younger kids have created a need for family-based therapy. In the past individual therapy would have sufficed, but today it is necessary for the entire family unit to attend. This is another instance where it's important for parents to participate fully in order for a complete healing process to take place.

In the book *Generation to Generation,* Rabbi Edwin Friedman provides a roadmap for clergy and leaders who are working with families that have experienced trauma.[80] Regardless of the family composition— single, blended, adopted, foster homes, separated, divorced, or cohabitating—the church is presented with the challenge of how to incorporate all parent figures in the healing and spiritual development process. In some ethnic-specific communities, clergy have earned the trust of families when it comes to addressing life issues more than professionals have. Other ethnic-specific communities avoid addressing family issues in public, which presents the church with another potential hindrance to engagement.

As families seek to heal together, family therapy in addition to counseling can become a golden spot for ministries, if embraced strategically. Ministries are increasingly offering Christian therapists to their ministry roster to support families desiring help through rough seasons. The church can serve as an agent of healing on many levels, spiritually and emotionally.

All Families?

In his book *The End of Youth Ministry?,* Andrew Root brings youth leaders on a journey to discover the "why" of youth ministry amidst the varied societal changes currently at play. Root challenges the congregation-based, middle-class youth ministry settings that have become "rudderless."[81] This journey readers take with Root brings to the surface many of the parental concerns with engagement specific to youth ministry (versus other social activities). The values of families inside and outside of the church have changed, but the church has not kept pace.

With this in mind, it's evident that in the next phase of youth ministry we must ask youth leaders to:

1. Discover the need to engage all families

2. Adjust and align its engagement according to the varied family structures

The starting point for all of this requires youth workers to have a clear picture of all families. Without one, the church is unable to participate in ministry to families. Note that I did not write "youth and their families." I am referring to "all families in general." Though over the years some churches have fared well in this area, the church as a whole has not been very successful in ministry to all families. In order to approach ministry in the best and most effective way, there must be an understanding of the purpose of family ministry. I think we can take the words of Dr. Chris Shirley as our focus: The church joins together to strengthen families and equip them to make disciples of Jesus Christ.[82]

Churches continue to face challenges when it comes to adapting to ever-changing social and family structures. As Shirley notes,

> We cannot keep changing the definition of family since scripture itself acknowledges varied family situations but the core teachings about the family remains consistent. Organizing and implementing family ministry with a clear definition of family allows leaders to advocate for God's best plan while applying the ministry of compassion, restoration and redemption as families struggle to reach the mark.[83]

Television shows like *Modern Family* and *This is Us* are pushing at the traditional definitions of family, thereby creating new mental models. As churches seek to engage all families, some of these family structures may not align with the traditional family models. Youth and church leaders will need to evaluate their current mental models about what types of families are worthy of their ministries. Different strategies and models will be necessary to truly engage all families.

By all means, be clear about your church's theological stance on these issues. Some youth leaders, for one example of why this matters, have not reckoned with the importance of reaching the entire family. These ministries focus on the young person, with little to no communication with the parents other than obtaining a permission slip for an upcoming trip. At the same time, other youth leaders are learning how to effectively minister to youth with the entire family in mind. We must continue to do this work. I'm not asking you to change what

Christ has taught us. I am asking you to consider what constitutes "all families." Are you willing to help a family that may be from a different ethnic group than your ministry with a food insecurity? What about the family with a child who is questioning their sexual identity? Can leaders walk alongside a family and help them to love unconditionally? The church will need to decide if *every family really means every family*, no matter its exact description. Once all families are valued, engagement will look very different.

A Pathway Forward for Increased Family Engagement

Now is an ideal, and critical, time to address these issues. As Kara Powell writes,

> With attendance tougher to assess, now is an ideal time to adopt new, creative metrics of success that better reflect our mission and goals of discipleship. During this pandemic, let's keep measuring students' attendance at online events, but let's also start tracking how their relationships with mentors and parents grow, how they tangibly serve others, and how they seek God all week. Shifting what we measure in the present will change our church culture in the future.[84]

Each ministry should develop a strategy for increasing family engagement from all families within its reach. Without an agreed-upon strategy that is communicated, periodically evaluated, and adjusted as needed, it will be difficult to assess if your ministry is effective in reaching all families. I believe there are four pillars necessary for building family engagement:

1. Identify Motives for Reaching ALL Families

2. Create Intentional Parental Connections

3. Form School Partnerships

4. Look for Ways to Provide Personal Touches

1. Identify Motives for Reaching ALL Families

In the book *Engage Every Family: Five Simple Principles*, which is aimed at engaging families in the educational lives of children, Steven M. Constantino invites public school educators to begin with an activity of asking a few questions to surface the personal starting point of each reader.[85] We as a church need to do something similar to truly assess each of our starting points.

It's easy for a church to say, "Of course we want to reach all families," but unless we address our individual and collective motives, we are likely to fail at doing so. Church and ministry leaders need to really examine the "why" behind their service to families. I would suggest creating a set of questions that address the compositions of the families that may come to your church to ask each church leader and youth leader. If you discover some resistance, fears, or even subtle hostility toward certain types of families, it may be helpful to engage some focus groups prior to reaching out to all families.

This step requires the church to do its research, such as learning from various ethnic groups through books, videos, podcasts, etc. You can also reach out to other churches and build relationships, asking questions of other youth leaders. Don't assume you know or understand. Be willing to be a learner and begin again. Suspend all judgment, especially based on past experiences.

2. Intentional Parental Connections

One of the pathways to increase family engagement is to establish a relationship with each family within the first three months of them attending your ministry. Once a teenager attends youth group three times, a home visit should be conducted. As you approach this step, keep in mind that social workers are great resources as they are trained to conduct home visits, and have a list of things to look for on their intake forms. Churches can create a similar list of information beyond basic demographics in order to understand the youth and families in their ministries.

Once the initial contact is made with a parent, the youth leader who first formed the relationship with the teenager can request to make a home visit. Most families will be surprised and excited to meet the youth leader. After this visit happens, the youth leaders can create and share a family profile that includes basic demographic information on the family and notes any specific details (items to collect in your database could include birthdays, favorite foods, family structure, known family stressors, etc.). Collecting and following up using this information can help you build relationships and help the ministry team to effectively serve each family in a holistic manner.

During the visit, youth generally give a tour of their home with the highlight being showing off their room. The personality of the teenager shines forth, giving the youth leader a clearer understanding of the heart and world of the young person. Parents like to take these visits as time to ask questions about the ministry and the youth leader's personal life. Parents begin to open up when they discover that the youth leader cares about their child and their family, and really wants to help them be a better parent.

Some youth leaders do not value family engagement and continue to do ministry without parents, missing the opportunity for the church to engage with the family in the healing and spiritual development process. Home visits are a vital tool for any youth leader who desires to create intentional parental connections. Be creative with parental connections. There are many resources available to help you in this area that are considerate of your context. One example is Orange, a ministry that believes that two combined influences in a child's life (such as the church and the family) make a greater impact than just two individual influences. Orange provides resources that help parents become more intentional with their child's spiritual development.[86]

3. Increased School Partnerships
In addition to home visits, it is important to conduct visits to each student's school. It is a good idea for the church to have a vested interest in the public schools that are educating the youth of the church. This should occur after the initial stage of the relationship is built with the parent because permission is needed to visit their school.

Be mindful of how students describe the youth leader to their school friends. Some students are clear about their faith while others will be less open. There is nothing like a school visit from your youth leader to raise the stakes for a young person who attends your youth group!

Feedback can be provided to parents after the school visit. This can be as simple as saying, "Thank you for connecting me to your son's/

daughter's school. It was fun to have lunch with him/her! I'd love to visit again in the future." This helps to deepen the relationship, and also opens the door for providing assistance that might be appreciated in the future with connecting parents to resources or support for their student.

Many schools, especially those in urban areas, are open to relationships with local churches. Youth have varied needs for mentorship and tutoring, and some just need additional adults in their daily lives.

4. Personal Touches

Young people need to grow up knowing they were made in the image of God and loved by Jesus so they can love others. But they may never understand what that looks like in action unless they have a few adults who demonstrate what it means to move beyond The Shallow Way.[87]

Youth leaders are some of the most creative people on the planet! I have learned and borrowed ideas for youth ministry that have helped to create my unique personal touch on the lives of youth and families in our ministry. Personal touches consist of the things you and your ministry do to help families feel a sense of belonging to your tribe. It can be as simple as always remembering each person's name, celebrating birthdays, and reaching out when they miss a week.

Youth and families know when you care. The personal touches that work in one environment may not translate to another. Be prayerful and watchful for the needs of your families. Each family touch, as these connections can be called, should involve a conversation and a prayer request from the family. Youth leaders can pray for specific requests from a family member. Sometimes the request will come from the youth themselves. Prayer must remain your constant focus regardless of the level of engagement.

Parental engagement will vary by family. Some families will not accept the invitation for a home or school visit. Always respect the will of the family. Others will welcome you with open arms and may go as far as including youth leaders at the school's parent-teacher conferences. The more you engage in the life of the family, the more the relationships deepen.

Yes, ALL Families

My church determined that ministry to all families meant each family we encountered should be strengthened, equipped, healed, and restored by our ministry. This mindset made it easier for us to leave the four walls of the building and meet families where they were. The goal was no longer to engage families inside the building but simply to engage families—all families. Our church became known for its sending capacity and not its seating capacity. The ministry's reach goes well beyond the people we see on Sundays, adjusting its thinking to engage all families during every day of the week. We aim to be creative in how we support and equip families.

Research still shows that parents remain the number one influence (positive or negative) in the lives of youth. Reggie Joiner understands all too well the importance of the family. He believes that in order to have a positive influence in the spiritual development of kids, churches should engage every parent.[88] The church cannot shun relationships with parents and expect to have a long-term impact on a youth's spiritual development. Perhaps this is why so many students walk away from their faith post high school. The church has not shown interest in the holistic, lifelong journey of their families.

All families need a personal touch from Christ. The church is the vehicle designed to give that touch. Let's reach all families.

Final Thoughts

At this point I may have raised more questions than answers for your context. Each church will need to consider its particular needs and touchpoints for the greatest leverage of engagement with families. Is your ministry designed to only connect with the stock photo family of mom, dad, and 2.5 kids? It is time to flip to a new page in the photo album, especially if you're trying to reach ethnic families in an urban environment. Look for new ways to build on the familial relationships that already exist within your community as you move beyond the minivan definition of family to embrace a more biblical, bus-sized view.

Creative engagement outside of the norm due to the season of COVID-19 has produced some amazing global models of family engagement. However, some youth leaders have not shifted their

attention to families and are still focused on youth individually.
We must continue to go where families are: schools, marketplaces,
supermarkets, the highways and the byways. Be visible in courthouses,
community events, health clinics, hospitals—any place families gather.

Youth leaders, your role is still important. While some theologians
and church leaders disagree with the need for a professional youth
leader, I would argue that they are needed now more than ever. The
training and development of youth leaders needs to be adjusted to
equip churches to successfully minister to all families. Many youth
leaders are trained to create and run programs for youth but not how to
strengthen, equip, heal, and restore families. These are essential needs
that must be met.

The family is a system that is interconnected with multiple external
systems that affect youth. The church must take the approach of Jesus
and include those who are securing the well-being of youth as part
of the larger family community. When I was growing up, my family
was surrounded by the church, not just a segment of the church.
Simultaneously, the adults and youth in my family formed a spiritual
community that connected with our church on many levels. Those
relationships kept my family healthy and spiritually growing, even as
my parents were in the process of a divorce.

I believe the biblical model of family is inclusive of any prototype of
family society can create. The church must follow the first and second
commandments of Christ: love God with all of your heart, soul, mind,
and strength, then love your neighbor as yourself. Youth ministry
that engages the redefined family will have a clear expected family
contribution that includes the following:

1. Sees the family

2. Loves the family

3. Strengthens, equips, heals, and restores the family

The family challenges we face were also present in biblical times:
blended families, orphans, etc. How will we equip the parents who
don't have or know their expected family contribution? The church
should not say to all families, "You don't fit this profile, so we don't

know how to equip and strengthen you. We cannot disciple you, lead you, and assist with your spiritual growth." So how can the church equip families who may never fit the traditional definition of family?

Our mental models of family can no longer consist of strictly middle-class, white, suburban, two-parent homes. A broader view enables us to be open to and serve whomever, however. It begs us to sing along with Mr. Rogers, *won't you please, won't you please, please won't you be my neighbor.* Jesus asked this question in his day: *Who is a neighbor to the one who fell among thieves?* The reply: *the one who showed mercy.* Jesus asks us to go and do likewise.

Family is and will continue to be the foundation stone of society, and ministry to the family must remain a priority on the church's agenda, not a goal relegated to youth ministry professionals. The social definition of family may change again. May the people of faith remain true to God's Word.

HOW I'M DOING THIS

RODRIGO AZEVEDO

I work for a Brazilian congregation in Marlboro, Massachusetts, a town about thirty minutes from Boston. Our community is focused on Brazilian immigrants because they are the majority of our congregation, with very few exceptions. To understand our youth ministry, it is necessary to understand the immigrant family and their socioeconomics.

The majority of these immigrants' stories are very similar. People immigrate seeking better opportunities, a better future for themselves and their families. Usually, these are people with low socioeconomic statuses and basic school instruction, people who did not have much prosperity in Brazil, often because of the lack of job opportunities. Consequently, they suffered from financial stresses, which led them to leave their home country.

Once they are here, parents work around sixty to eighty hours per week, trying to pay off the debts that they made coming to the US while also doing their best to provide for their families. To meet the financial need, in two-parent homes both parents have to work, leaving youth alone. Parents and children do not have time together and as a consequence they often do not know what is happening in each other's lives. Even those immigrants who have been here longer and have paid off their immigration-related debts keep working the same long hours because their jobs are low-paying and they dream of going back to Brazil one day, which never comes. This cycle repeats year after year. The majority of these immigrants are undocumented (do not have legal status) and do not speak English, which aggravates the problems already mentioned. The result is that youth are left to raise themselves with little supervision and help.

All these factors affect youth ministry in many ways, but I will point to just a few. First, parents' involvement in the church is almost nonexistent, and it is hard to find volunteers. Second, parents are always worried about financial problems, which consume their thoughts and time, leaving no room to think about how to raise their kids. Third, these parents generally expect the church and the youth team to give youth everything they need to grow in their relationship with God.

The family format is also not very "traditional" in many cases. Dr. Ward's diverse family picture is very accurate among these immigrants. Many live with just a mom or a dad because their parents divorced after they arrived. Others live with grandparents or uncles. Yet others live by themselves in a friend's house or rent a room.

The question is, how can we help in this situation? Is there any hope?

Yes, there is. Against all odds, our ministry has experienced significant growth in the last seven years, which can be attributed to many factors. I will restrain my writing to just the youth group itself.

Our group has jumped from twelve youth seven years ago to around eighty today. First, we meet every Friday night, sometimes with many people and sometimes with few. But no matter what, we are there. Second, we have partnerships with other ministries in the church. Youth feel they are part of the larger church and useful to it. This motivated us as we started a program to create a youth worship band that leads worship every Friday; many teenagers are now also part of the church's worship team. Every Wednesday, our pastor leads a big theatrical group made up of mostly youth, with the addition of a few parents and children, training them to proclaim the Bible through arts. This is a great way to involve parents and youth in the same ministry. Our church's media ministry is made up of many teens, young adults, and parents. We also have a youth dance ministry. All of these ministries exist to involve youth in the church, making them feel part of the congregation and the family of God. One result is that many parents come to church because of their children's interest in being there.

Once we've connected with youth, we seek to understand their stories and know them better: where they came from (this is very important because Brazil is a huge and diverse country), their family structure and living situation, and why they came to the US and, later, to our church. Some parents introduce us to their children, hoping that they'll get involved with the group. These parents are easy to develop further conversations with. But some young people come without parents, and we only get to know those parents after a time. This second group is a little more difficult to get involved in the church, but not impossible.

A holistic approach to youth group has to involve families. Our experience is that the youth whose families are also connected have a more secure faith, are more involved in the church, and are often more optimistic about life in general. Conversely, when the family is not involved, youth tend to be less connected with the church and youth group, and tend to engage in more problematic behaviors. We are called to help youth and their families grow in God's likeness and to help them build better relationships both inside and outside their homes. Families are vital to the success of our ministry.

Rodrigo Azevedo *is a youth leader at Bethel Presbyterian Church in Marlborough, MA, and is also planting a church among the Brazilian immigrant community in Lowell, MA. He holds a M.Div. from Gordon-Conwell Theological Seminary and is currently finishing a Th.M. in New Testament.*

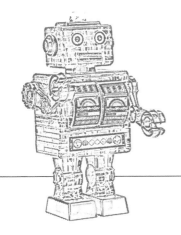

VIEW 5:
REFLECTIONS FROM THIS SIDE OF THE POND: OUR REALITY AND YOUR FUTURE?

BY CHRIS CURTIS

The day I got back from my last trip to the States in 2018, I sat talking in the afternoon sun with a group of fantastic young people at a youth center near where I live, just north of London. I was impressed, as I often am, by their animated conversations about everything from music to US politics to climate change. I can't remember being that engaged with the world when I was fifteen. One of them, Owen, said to me, "The Americans are more religious, aren't they? They're into God, not like us."

Hoping Owen was talking about nations and not making a judgement about the two of us, I agreed, at least as a very broad generalization. There are many places I've visited in the US where church attendance and Christian faith are still very much at the heart of the community—and of course there are plenty of others where they are not. Nevertheless, I think the general point holds. The UK is further along in the progression of secularization than the US. The draining of religious faith from every aspect of society is well underway here. The UK is not necessarily anti-Christian, it just sees Christians and Christianity as, well, irrelevant. Gen Z—young people born after 1996—are becoming teenagers in a quantifiably different religious climate. Dr. Sarah Williams memorably calls it "spiritual climate change," a fundamental shift in the missional environment of our nation, and she reminds us of Jesus's call in Mark 16 for us to read the "signs of the times."[89] Just over a century ago, 80% of young teens attended Sunday School.[90] I'll tell you in a moment where we are today. In the meantime, you might like to take a guess.

For all the differences between our nations, there's enough in common to perhaps think of us in the UK as a kind of giant R&D lab for the challenges in youth ministry heading your way. Our experiences are worth studying because they may be your experiences very shortly. Perhaps sooner than you think. "We're twenty years behind you when it comes to young people and Christian faith!" said one youth pastor on that trip to the US. We were standing outside a church in Williamsburg, New York. I paused, and that moment in Jurassic Park came to mind when the T. rex is chasing down the Jeep and its menacing jaws are reflected in the side-view mirror ("objects in mirror are closer than they appear"). If you think you have twenty years to come to terms with what we in the UK are experiencing, you are in for a shock. Culture is shifting much faster than that. If there are going to be any comparisons between what is happening here in the UK and what is coming in the US, then don't imagine you have that long to adjust to them.

So what has this shift meant for youth ministry in the UK, and what challenges does it present for the next decade? Of course, we're not a single homogeneous entity any more than the US. Our areas include the rural, very rural (The Scottish Highlands!), suburban, and inner city. There is growing ethnic diversity, at least in some regions. There are thriving cities with affluence on brash display, but also rapidly increasing poverty. It's a bit of everything you have, but on a smaller scale and with a little more rain.

There are some 50,000 churches in the UK. The established denominations, of course, but also plenty of what we sometimes call "fresh expressions," new churches meeting in everything from school halls to repurposed pubs. But old or new, one thing is common to almost all of them: a decline in youth ministry.

"Decline" is putting it politely. In fact, youth ministry just doesn't happen any more in three quarters of those churches. There is no provision for middle or high school age during a service. No midweek youth group, no youth choir. No uniformed group centered around Christian values like Boys' Brigade. Nothing for youth in three out of four churches. That 80% or so of young teens attending church just over a century ago? Now it has shrunk to an estimated 2% and it's still falling. In some of the older, traditional denominations, youth ministry is almost extinct. The COVID-19 pandemic and months of lockdown only served to accelerate this process. Of course, there is still amazing youth ministry going on up and down the UK, but it doesn't hide the devastating decline we're experiencing.

This isn't just statistics. Here's how it plays out: I'm sitting with Darren, a fourteen-year-old boy, in his front room in a down-at-heel part of town with large households crammed in small houses squashed together in row after row of homes built for an industrial boom a century ago and now a testament to what happens when there is an economic bust. Darren is cheeky and immensely likeable. His attendance at school is erratic—which is why I'm there. He harbors deep and unspoken hurt at how the father who moved out when he was eight now lives a mile away with a new woman and new child. The hurt comes out in other ways, often in fights with peers and teachers. Darren needs love and care, trusted adults who'll walk this difficult path with him. But there's a problem. Sitting there in his front room, we're less than 500 yards from four churches. None of them has any youth ministry.

I know there are thousands of young people like Darren whom the church could and should be serving. It's devastating knowing we are not. Despite that, I do have a sense of hope about the future. In the words of Paul, we are hard-pressed on every side, but not crushed. How so?

What's dying in the face of secularization are our methods. The way we've done youth ministry for the last quarter century. And maybe good riddance. It seems we were reluctant to let them go, but the changes I'm describing have done the dirty work for us. Now it's time for us to change, too.

Change is difficult. People often talk a good game about it, but let's not kid ourselves that it's easy. Change in the church may be even more difficult. If you decide to do something new as a youth pastor, you still have to bring the church leadership, parents, and everyone else along with you. Charles Kettering, the famous American inventor and engineer, put it nicely when he said, "People are open minded about new things—as long as they're like the old ones."[91] If you've ever made a presentation to the church about youth ministry, you'll appreciate Kettering's witty insight. Just move the night your youth group meets and you'll likely face a tsunami of complaints from parents. What if you need to change something more fundamental?

Whatever the challenges, the pace of change in our society is increasing, and it's brought us to the point in the UK where we can't carry on any longer with youth ministry in its present form. Change is urgent. We've run out of time.

This is good news.

Change is a moment of challenge for the church, but it is also the moment of opportunity for the gospel. Think of Jesus's followers at the beginning of the story of Acts. Their horizon barely extended beyond the walls of Jerusalem, where they were huddled together in a single room. But a great persecution breaks out and they are scattered not just across Israel but into Samaria and then into completely new worlds: Phoenicia, Cyprus, and Antioch. The implication is that were it not for the persecution, they might never have made those journeys, learned those new languages, adapted to those new cultures, and found themselves a million miles from the safety and familiarity of that Upper Room.

That's the journey I believe we're about to embark upon in the UK.

The challenges we face can transform us into something wild and different and exciting. New journeys, new languages, new places. Out of the church vestry where we've been meeting for the last goodness knows how many years. Out of the preplanned curriculum that packages together ready-to-consume content far too neatly. Out of the models of discipleship and evangelism that we've become comfortable with even though we know they stopped really working a generation or more ago.

Out with the old, in with the new.

There are going to be some challenges along the way. I want to talk about the three of them that I consider to be the most pressing. By implication, even if they're not part of your experience right now in the US, they may reflect what you will be facing soon. Objects in mirror are closer than they appear.

Making Connections:
Youth Ministry When Young People Are Absent

The places where the church traditionally met and built relationships with young people are disappearing—and it's not clear what spaces can replace them.

Mission is a fundamental part of youth ministry. In my first days as a youth pastor—we're talking in the eighties and nineties, mind you—we went door to door inviting youth to attend our weekly gatherings and one-off events, and we held youth services at church. We hired touring groups of Christian bands, drama companies, and dance troupes, and we staged concerts. We made presentations in schools (you can do that kind of thing here) and took young people from the local community to summer camps. It was fruitful—and fun.

But now those spaces are shifting or disappearing altogether. Jean Twenge, one of the leading academic commentators on young people and social media, contends that young people are simply leaving the house less. They're hanging out with their friends, yes, but it's online by social media, chat, or through a shared game. They have access, at a moment's notice, to billions of hours of entertainment on YouTube and Netflix. In short, they don't need to turn up at our events to connect with their friends and have fun.[92]

We see that in stark terms in the UK. Just down the road from me is a church that for years has run a typical Friday evening youth group. It's attracted not only the young people from the church but a steady stream from the community. Some are friends of the church kids, some just turned up and got involved. The format has been common to thousands of groups across the UK for decades. A group is kicking a Nerf football around the hall, there are games out, and sometime toward the end of the evening everyone will gather together for some kind of input—a game introducing a theme, a talk, a discussion, a prayer. As much as anything, this kind of group is a place for young people in the community to connect with the church, get to know the adult volunteers and youth leaders, and perhaps end up coming on the church youth weekend. It's messy but it's mission.

But over the last decade these groups have grown younger (as older teens dismissed it as an option in favor of Starbucks or chatting online) and then in size (as the attraction for even younger teens faded). Those groups are rare these days. I'm not suggesting they were the most innovative, but at least they were a space where you met young people beyond the church family. How do you meet fifteen-year-olds in your local community today? Figuring that out is the challenge we face. Schools are much less open to local Christian youth workers visiting— it happens, but more and more it's focused on providing voluntary pastoral work like mentoring, rather than proclamation. Twenty years ago, most high schools would have had regular group assemblies with a religious theme, and invited people like me in to speak at them. Now, even though that theoretically is still a requirement, these types of assemblies and invitations have largely disappeared. Other contexts for meeting young people have also diminished—summer youth camps have never been as popular as in the US, but fell even more out of favor. Did I mention the rain?

You'd imagine that as things changed, we'd redouble our efforts in new and creative forms of evangelism, especially when we're at 2% of young people and falling. But instead, something rather counterintuitive happened: We focused more and more on the young people we already had in our groups instead. Discipleship has become the central theme of youth ministry, and evangelism plays at best a secondary role.

There are other factors pushing us in this direction. Numbers of paid youth workers have fallen by about 50% and increasingly youth ministry is led by volunteers. Some interesting UK research indicates little difference in the effective discipleship of young people in the church whether led by a paid worker or volunteer.[93] Where it does have an impact is in missional activities, which occur much less in volunteer-led groups, for understandable reasons. Volunteers often have less capacity and time available. In many cases the volunteers may be parents of the young people in the group, so it's no surprise the focus is on the young people you have, not those beyond the church.

All of this means that at the very point when evangelism is more vital than ever, we're doing less of it than ever. We can challenge those young people in the church to bring their friends, of course, but when numbers are already small it doesn't shift the overall pattern—assuming the young people in our churches are even interested in inviting their friends. We can try to engage young people online but, in my view, that's proving much more difficult than we might have imagined.

No, we have to rethink mission in youth ministry in bolder and bigger ways. But this challenge is easy to avoid if we instead circle the wagons and concentrate on discipling the young people in the church. The same often is seen in adult congregations in decline where, often without realizing it, churches move into survival mode, concentrating on running the basic functions of the church, like Sunday services. Ironically this is anything but survival mode; rather it locks them into a cycle of decline where, with fewer people, they lose the capacity to do mission. That's what's happening in youth ministry in the UK. We are focusing on the ones we have.

Creating Curiosity:
Youth Ministry in an Age of 'Meh'

Here's the second challenge we'll face in the 2020s. Secularization and modern life have deadened curiosity about the spiritual and about Christian faith. It's not gone, but it's buried under a thick layer of twenty-first century life.

We asked a group of young people in the UK what their big questions were about faith and the meaning of life. This group was drawn from a wide representation of backgrounds, ethnicities, and faiths, but their answers were remarkably consistent: They had no questions! Nada. No questions about God, no deep musings about where we come from, nothing about what lies beyond. No curiosity.

111

Curiosity is interest that leads to inquiry. It's what took Alice down the rabbit hole, but it's also what helps start people on a journey to faith. A burning question, a nagging doubt, a deep longing. It's what makes you join an Alpha group (small group), or turn up at a church service, or simply debate religion with your friends.

Curiosity is a natural human trait. It isn't about immediate need, like hunger or thirst; it's a deeper craving to know and understand. "Every bit of human progress, that's ever been made, occurred because somebody was curious about doing things in a new or different or combination-with-something-else way," said the late astronaut John Glenn.[94] "The important thing is not to stop questioning…never lose a holy curiosity," Albert Einstein counseled in 1955.[95]

Curiosity drives scientific discovery, but it's also what compels people to explore questions of faith. It's what drove me as a teenager, like so many others, to turn up at a youth group and eventually utter one of those "so if you're up there, show yourself to me now!" kinds of prayers. "I need to know one way or the other!" Turned out I got an answer, and the rest is, well, you know.

One of the biggest challenges we in the UK face in Christian mission is the draining of spiritual curiosity from people's lives. Back to those young people we interviewed—each for a whole hour. What did they really want to know about the existence (or not) of God, what lies beyond death, or simply what is the meaning of this life?

Nothing.

Strikingly, none of them had any burning questions.

Here's Brook: "I don't think anything. I just don't believe in God. Never thought about that."

And Sophie, in response to the interviewer asking what questions she had about God, faith, and religion: "No, nothing." The interviewer tries again. "Nothing you want to ask or talk about?" Sophie: "No, there's nothing at all."

Welcome to youth ministry in an age of "meh."

We're working in a decade where the majority of young people aren't going to be spiritually curious. Back when I started youth ministry in the 1980s and 1990s, we used to hold special events in schools—remember, the UK has traditionally allowed Christians to visit and run groups and clubs in schools—that we'd call "Grill a Christian." Come and ask any question you have about faith, no matter how tricky, and we'll do our best to answer it. Hands down, these were the best-attended meetings we'd hold in the year. The place would be packed. The gladiatorial style of questioning helped for sure, but there was also a natural curiosity toward Christianity and whether it could make sense of the world. Fast forward to these events today, and the room is practically empty. Young people just aren't spiritually curious and it's presenting some new challenges for mission and youth ministry.

It's worth asking why this is happening. I have a couple of working theories. The first is the deadening effect of secularization that has driven faith out of everyday life. You don't see it anymore, and out of sight, out of mind. Gone are religious television programs—or if they're not gone, they're at least relegated to some obscure cable channels. Gone are the norms of attending church on major holidays like Christmas or Easter. You'd be hard pressed to find an Advent Calendar that has any kind of religious theme. Religious funerals and religious weddings are in steep decline, so you might never be invited to one. The falling off in numbers of practicing Christians over many decades has gotten to the point where you might not know anyone with Christian faith. There's simply little or no opportunity to come across Christianity in day-to-day life.

That's even more the case for young people. Yes, there are Christian videos on YouTube, and a bunch of ministries dedicated to making them, but they're outnumbered roughly 10:1 by videos on cats and nearly 20:1 by videos on makeup! We're an obscure minority interest at best.

In the everyday lives of young people, faith exists now only in faint echoes: A Nike advertisement that uses religious imagery, a cross as a piece of jewelry, a cuss word. But those few references are drowned out by everything else.

Secularization is, of course, more than removing the visual presence of religion in society. It brings excessive individualism, where technology and science are seen as the gateway to human flourishing. It flattens life to the immediate, the consumable, the tangible. The mystery of faith seems little more than a human coping mechanism. Grow up in that world and no wonder you have few, if any, questions about the divine.

Perhaps there are also practical reasons for this absence of curiosity in young people. Always online, every moment of the day can be filled with a meme or video or social media post. There's no downtime, no opportunity for reflection, for even as you drift off the sleep it is likely that your phone is beside you, the last thing you see at night, and the first thing you'll pick up in the morning. The loud, the urgent, the bright crowd out everything else.

This is proving to be a real challenge for youth ministry. The timing could not have been worse. Forms of ministry that used entertainment to attract young people are increasingly viewed as shallow or, worse, manipulative. It's harder to compete for young people's attention. And if you want to go deeper with young people, to make youth ministry more substantial, how do you do that at the very point when interest in the "deep" is shallower than ever?

But still: There's hope, and more to tell about this concept of curiosity. Let me take you back to those young people we interviewed, because that story isn't quite finished. Each interview lasted an hour, and was taped and transcribed as part of the research. If you follow the conversations through, you'll see something quite amazing happen. Questions gradually begin to emerge. Little by little, each and every one of those young people began to rediscover their curiosity. The interview acted as a stimulant. The common thread at the end was "Can't we keep on talking…this is great…I want to talk about these ideas more!"

Listening to these conversations again is striking. It reminds me of a nature documentary set in a dry desert land. There's no life; seemingly nothing can exist or grow in the sand and heat. But then—and maybe you've seen some program like this too—there's rain. A monsoon. And overnight green shoots appear. Like magic, plants poke through the desert floor, and insects and animals emerge from hiding. Life was buried and asleep, not destroyed.

That's how I see young people in the UK. Sure, they have no spiritual questions. Except they do. They're just buried deep beneath a thick layer of cultural dust. Layers of secularization. And social media. And videos about make-up. The challenge for youth ministry in the next decade is to figure out how to get beneath that dust.

Restoring Credibility:
Youth Ministry When You've Lost Your Standing

The issues of contact and curiosity likely seem challenging enough on their own, but I've saved the biggest problem until last: our loss of credibility. The credibility of both the church and Christian faith, for the distinction between the two is invisible and irrelevant to those outside it. This lack of credibility has profound implications for presenting the gospel to young people in the coming decade.

In the eyes of the young, Christianity can no longer be relied upon as a sound source of identity and purpose. The broader context for this change is the failure and decline of modernism, the dominant thought structure of the last 300 years that began with the Enlightenment. Christianity enjoyed a position of power and privilege in this world, especially in the UK, where bishops sat in Parliament and the church was the center of social and cultural life in every village and town. Christian ideas and values were enshrined in law and in culture.

The certainties offered by modernism have failed to deliver. These certainties no longer seem plausible in light of the problems the world faces. The church barely has the means to describe the problems before us, let alone tackle them. In some cases, the church has even caused them. This has worrying implications for the church in the next decade. Dean Inge, the English priest and writer, put it starkly: "The church that marries the culture in one age becomes a widow in the next."[96] In the eyes of the young, we're the problem, not the answer.

That powerful underlying sense that the church is part of what got us to where we are today is fleshed out in a multiplicity of issues in politics, race, gender, and economics. When it comes to many of the problems in these areas, the church is perceived as silent, or complicit, or worse.

Climate is a good example. In 2021, Tearfund and Youthscape copublished a new piece of research about climate change and the church. You won't be surprised that tackling climate change is one of the most important world issues identified by young people.[97] But even young people growing up in the church see the church as ineffectual in addressing this challenge. In the eyes of young people, even as movements like Extinction Rebellion were holding protests on London streets and demanding change, churches were rather pleased with themselves for recycling their rubbish. Too little, too late, and nowhere near radical enough to make a difference. No Christian young person in the research had heard anyone address the issue from the pulpit, let alone felt the passion and urgency with which Wilberforce and the Clapham Sect tackled issues like slavery in earlier centuries. Think about that for a moment, because it's astonishing. No young person— and in this research, these are young people within the church—had heard anyone stand at the front of the service and talk about what many would describe as the greatest threat to humanity. No wonder young people in the church and beyond see the church as part of the establishment that got us into this mess, not as the radical message of hope you and I know it to be.

This is the overarching story. I know that there are churches that are different, and Christians who feel passion for these issues. I know the story is much more complex. But that's not the point, or at least not the point I'm making here. The good examples do not cancel out the bad. The bad examples are setting the story that young people across society are hearing and seeing. The same is being played out in those other arenas—in politics, race, gender, and economics. Wilberforce's scathing review of comfortable Christianity in his writings is sadly just as relevant at the decline of modernism as it was at its birth.

These challenges are not new. Young people have been leaving the church in the UK in growing numbers since at least the 1990s. But the scale and speed have accelerated, and we've passed a tipping point. Ask a young person in any town or city who can solve the challenges the world faces, who offers hope, and they will not name the church. Our credibility is gone, spent out. Hastened perhaps by other challenges like the sexual abuse scandals that mean every minister—or church youth worker—might be a suspected pedophile. No doubt such views flourish in the cold climate of secularism. It may not be completely fair, but it's fair enough to have traction.

Of course, those of us in the church know about the amazing and extensive ministry going on around the world to serve the poor, care for the orphan, and care for the sick. But I wonder if youth ministry, and the church as a whole, has become too removed from that work, and if that remove unintentionally contributes to our loss of credibility. Over the last fifty years there's been a proliferation of parachurch organizations tackling the described challenges. In combating poverty, for example, there are international Christian agencies at work all over the world, as well as nonprofits in every town and region of our own country. Same for climate change and many other urgent issues of the day.

There are logical and sensible reasons for setting up nonprofits to tackle society's problems. The concentration of expertise and skills and the capacity to work at scale make them much more effective. But there's an unintended consequence I wonder if you've thought about. This approach has the tendency to reduce the role of the local congregation to fundraising for these causes. We don't address poverty ourselves; we support a local charity that addresses poverty on our behalf. It makes much of the ministry of the church unwittingly invisible to us, including to young people. If you grow up in the church, or you just attend a youth group, you don't see what's going on. And what you don't see, you don't know about, or you forget about. In essence, we're deskilling young people to be activists and to change their world. Instead of putting on a sponsored car wash to raise money for a local cause, perhaps we should be equipping young people to address that injustice themselves? Gen Y were, in broad terms, interested in bettering themselves. What we're learning about Gen Z, in its early days, given that most of them are still young teens, is that they are more focused on the world and making a difference. Fundraising is a poor substitute for protesting with Extinction Rebellion, or serving the poor a meal, or helping someone find housing. This is our faith, right? So maybe the 2020s are the time to stop reducing the experience of that faith to something much less urgent and passionate. When it came to that research on climate change, what young people were frustrated with wasn't just that no one was talking about it in church services—that was just the starting point. They also wanted action.

The challenge of credibility is not going to be easy to overcome in the next decade, but if we are to engage young people, we will have to find a way.

What Now?

Where does this leave youth ministry in the UK? What will the 2020s look like? Continued decline or something new and more hopeful? How do we overcome the challenges we face? My answer is in the words of Paul in Corinthians: faith, hope, and love. These three are the key to how youth ministry might reimagine itself.

To an absence of connection, I offer faith.

To an absence of curiosity, I offer hope.

To an absence of credibility, I offer love.

Faith

To an absence of connection, I offer faith.

Let's start by saying we simply have to reconnect with young people in our communities. How can we live with ourselves if we don't? If youth ministry becomes just about discipling the young people we have, then it's gotten too small for me. And way too small for the gospel.

The motivation for this isn't to save the church. We don't need to renew our commitment to mission just to increase the numbers in our declining youth groups. We need to renew our commitment to mission because we believe that our faith is what makes sense of us and the world—and young people. Don't make the mistake of believing that mission will save the institution of the church—or to be more precise, the current embodiment of the church. That will pass. Rather, the next decade has to see a renewal of mission because we've rediscovered the fundamental call to take the message of Jesus far and wide, like those first followers in the early church.

This renewal of mission will mean not only finding new spaces in which to make contact with young people but also, I suggest, finding a different tone that connects with young people more deeply. Those spaces are going to be hard to come by. There's no magic new context that replaces the ones that are disappearing. We are going to have become creative: a pop-up in a local shop, an art display in a school entrance. These are the kinds of places youth workers are experimenting with now.

Even more important is what we talk about when we get there. My instinct is that mission in the next decade needs to be more directly about young people encountering God for themselves. By that I mean less events that talk about faith and more that direct young people to their own spiritual encounter and the presence of God. We've been experimenting with mission that asks young people to participate in prayer, to experience silence, to worship. Yes, these are the kinds of things we used to offer once you'd become a Christian. I think those experiences of faith may now be the best way to do mission. If we are to gain interest from young people in the gospel, we need to go deeper, not shallower. This will mean more authentic and serious conversation and engagement with young people than we've often had.

Hope
To the absence of curiosity, I offer hope.

Hope, in Christian terms at least, is certainty about the future, about who we are created to be, about what it means to be human. In his seminal work *A Secular Age*, Charles Taylor offers a lucid account of why the modern self is facing a moral crisis. He sees a threat from the elevation of science as the key to understanding human beings, reducing everything to the "biology of the brain."[98] He's not anti-science; instead, he argues for a richer, deeper understanding of the self that embraces something more mysterious and deep. The central question, according to Taylor, is not about the divine but about the self.[99]

If we are to reengage young people's curiosity, it will not be with questions about God, but with questions about what it means to be human. That's our new starting place. The traditional apologetic questions that dominated evangelism in my generation—Who was Jesus? What is the evidence for the existence of God?—are no longer where the conversation begins. Instead, we must discover a rich new dialogue about what it means to be human. And this is where Christian faith offers a compelling and different and quite beautiful vision. It doesn't exclude conversations about God, it's the path toward them. This is how we might hope to renew curiosity in Gen Z.

Remember too those conversations we had in our research. Over the course of an hour, curiosity emerged. It takes time to go deeper and connect with young people in a more fundamental way. We tried something recently that seemed a million miles away from the crazy zany youth events we used to run: We commissioned a wonderful artist to create manga-style images of the story of Job, sixty-six of them in total. We printed them out in giant format and created an art gallery to display them. We gave young people headphones and invited them to listen to excerpts of the story of Job as they walked around the softly lit studio, taking it in at their own pace. Job resonates with young people because it's not a neat story with an easy ending—it's a rich and complex tale that creates as many questions as it answers, a story that talks about humans and their experiences. I remember watching one young teen from the local community walk around. He'd come intrigued by what he'd seen through the window. There was an eerie silence to the place because everyone had headphones in, listening to the words of Job put to music. But I could see it captivated him: The story connected in ways that an old-style Bible talk might have missed. I was as mesmerized by watching him as he was by the artwork. I could see questions being formed in his mind. Curiosity. No wonder he wanted to sit and talk afterward.

"Curiouser and curiouser!" is Alice's famous cry in in Lewis Carroll's book. That's what I hope young people will be saying about faith if we can connect with their spoken and unspoken questions about what it means to be human.

Love
To the challenge of credibility, I offer love.

What else is there? There's no other way back from a loss of credibility than to love—to put others' interests before your own. This is not an instant answer because it takes time to rebuild trust. But it's the only way I can see of reengaging young people who are disillusioned with the church and Christian faith. Love alone is believable.

When we love young people, we find ourselves suddenly in a world where different priorities emerge. Our focus isn't on preserving the youth group and our own world, it's on others. We think about their mental health, their education and employment, the state of the natural world in which they are growing up. Love switches the agenda from ourselves and what we want to do to the needs of others.

A group of youth leaders—a few hundred in total—were asked what themes they'd tackled in their youth ministry in the previous twelve months. A remarkably coherent list emerged, and it featured heavily on Christian doctrine, the value of Bible study and of church. Here's the twist. A group of young people in those churches was asked what themes they wanted their youth group to tackle. You won't be surprised at their list. It was essentially an upside-down version of the one from the youth leaders. The themes at the very bottom of the youth leaders' list were at the top of the young people's—and vice versa.[100]

Even if you accept that there are things you want to talk about that young people may not see as a priority (I'm not suggesting Christian doctrine is not important), the overall impression is hard to ignore. When you talk about what you want to talk about, not what young people want to talk about…how is that love? Love starts with the person in front of you, not with your own agenda. If we are going to restore credibility with young people, we have to start talking about what matters to them. Climate, identity, mental health, jobs, gender, and so on.

Love demands a change in how we have those conversations. Ever since the Sunday School offered young people an alternative to the main church service, the basic model of youth ministry has been rooted in education. We are the teacher. Young people are the students. Think about how much the language and philosophy of education pervades youth ministry. We have curriculum. We teach lessons. We divide young people up using the language of schools—middle school, high school. No amount of games or interactivity can hide the basic dynamic of what we really think youth ministry is all about.

That dynamic now needs to change. Love sees young people differently. And the educational model of youth ministry isn't a great way to do that. Gen Z needs something different.

A practical example might help. What about a Bible study journal that is only sold in packs of two—one for the young person and one for the youth leader? You study together and compare notes. You learn from each other. The young person learning from (hopefully) the wisdom and insights of the youth leader. But the youth leader learning from the fresh insights of the young person. It's a little idea, but it's a big leap in thinking from the way much of youth ministry has worked.

I'm convinced that love renews how we see others, which in turn reshapes what we do with them. This kind of thinking can be as radical as you dare. But it's the only path back to credibility with this generation of young people.

And Here's Where We Start

To begin this journey, I'd like to suggest we start with prayer. I'll admit that it's hard to do that when facing so many challenges. In the modernistic world in which I grew up, prayer was often treated as a prelude to action. You prayed before you ate, talked, acted. It was the starter before the main course—which was action and strategy and programs.

That's the temptation I face now. To conjure up a thousand strategies to meet the challenges I've outlined. To imagine that I am going to solve this through some clever innovation. That's nonsense, of course. The starting point isn't a shiny new program, it's to rediscover our call to be followers of Christ. Prayer isn't functional; it's not a means to an end. Communion with Jesus is the end! To meet culture at a moment of change requires a revitalization of our relationship with Jesus.

There is no other way. The One we follow has seen many dramatic transformations in cultures and continents. He has led the church through them, those who would follow, and he will lead us through this one. I don't mean to be glib, but a rediscovery of prayer might just be the key to seeing what God is doing in the next decade and how to join in.

We are hard pressed on every side, but not crushed; perplexed, but not in despair.[101] The future of youth ministry could be its most radical reinvention in a century. I'm hopeful about what we'll see in the UK, and pray our experiences might inform what's ahead for you in the US.

HOW I'M DOING THIS

PAUL CABLE

It's the second week of the third national lockdown in the UK. Ensuring that my top half is presentable whilst sporting a pair of trackie bottoms ("sweatpants") below the camera-line I log myself onto our virtual youth gathering. Before COVID we would have met in person with up to twenty young people to play games and have conversations around faith and life. Our ministry's pre-pandemic situation of having paid staff, space, volunteers, and young people turning up is becoming increasingly rare in the UK context, and it's a joy to be part of. Having joined the church only eighteen months ago I am so grateful for all those who came before me to lay the foundations of this ministry, yet I also feel an intense amount of pressure to maintain those kinds of numbers.

That evening, four young people logged on.

This pressure and anxiety around keeping things going so that young people keep turning up has driven many of my youth ministry decisions. It is a mentality enforced by well-meaning church members who ask, "How is the youth ministry going?" and in the same breath ask, "…and how many are you getting?" Numbers can be a helpful indicator of the health of a ministry, but more often they reveal an underlying anxiety. The focus on numbers as a sign of health is a recipe for burnout and disappointment, and it also masks the underlying issue: one of spiritual decline.

Chris points out that youth ministry in the UK has largely focused on discipleship from within the church rather than evangelism to those outside. I agree wholeheartedly with his assertion that this needs to shift. However, youth ministers regularly come up against obstacles. Firstly, churches are often unwilling to change and adapt so that young people can participate within the community's worshipping life. Secondly, the youth workers are already engaged in evangelism—only it's to young people within the faith community itself. Attendance at church isn't necessarily an indicator of a resilient faith. In fact, our pursuit of cultural relevance in youth ministry has often meant inviting young people into something that doesn't look all that different from the surrounding secular culture.

Youth ministry tends to be isolated and separated from the wider church ministry. Despite the inherent difficulty this presents, these obstacles require a whole-church response. Chris highlights the urgency of the need for change. We, rather, seem to be continuing to rearrange deck chairs on the Titanic instead of repenting of the ways secularism has crept into our churches.

What might an alternative look like? Chris suggests responding in faith, hope, and love. Faith is an excellent starting point, as it is about "abandoning all trust in one's own resources... Faith implies complete reliance on God and full obedience to God."[102] Many youth workers in my wider circles are attempting to replace the narrative of crisis with this narrative of faith. Instead of asking where the other twenty are when four young people log on, we are learning to ask, *What might God be doing in this?* Pastor and author Mark Sayers writes, "What if this secular moment in our culture is only a crisis if we ignore God's call for renewal? What if we reframe this as brilliantly good news? God always has His people where He wants His people. With nothing to turn to but Him."[103]

What if the current decline of young people is actually God's answer to reconnecting the church with young people? What if we saw the few young people who did turn up as a creative minority and worked alongside them toward renewal and revival? Those four young people who logged on, they have been consistent throughout the pandemic. Moreover, they have a genuine hunger for God, and they want to know what he is doing about global issues and how they can join in with his mission. Why should this faithful and hopeful small group of young people be sidelined by a ministry playing the numbers game? Especially since in God's economy it is usually the many who end up benefiting and being blessed by the few (Jesus worked with twelve!).

In my contexts, we have begun to shift from talking about doing ministry *for* young people, to doing ministry *with* young people. Our vision is to see our youth groups be powerhouses for spiritual and social renewal in church and society. As Chris writes, "the dynamic now needs to change. Love sees young people differently." We need to see young people not in terms of educational models but as active participants within the mission of God, people we can work and serve alongside. In practice our meetings are beginning to look more like "think tanks" or "creative innovation labs" rather than lessons. We are learning to pray together and be led by the Spirit to transform church and society and to reach out to the disconnected. For me, a weight is lifting as we venture into this. Instead of anxiously worrying about low numbers, I am beginning to see who has shown up!

Paul Cable is a youth worker in Salisbury (England) and is passionate about pioneering new ways of engaging young people with Jesus and his church. Paul loves books, movies, and getting outdoors with the family. He thinks and writes about youth ministry with friends at www.youthworkproject.com.

APPENDIX

KENDA CREASY DEAN

Re-Weirdifying Youth Ministry: Case Studies

Publisher's note: When Kenda Dean turned in the draft of her chapter, she included multiple examples of ministries that were embodying the content. We found these fascinating and helpful, but including them made her chapter significantly longer than the others, so we've made the call to share them with you here as an appendix. Enjoy!

Down Is Up:
Growing Change (Wagram, North Carolina)

The most obvious sign of an upside-down youth ministry is its "turn the tables" quality—taking a zombie practice and turning it over to become something else. Zombies, as it turns out, aren't just undead B-movie characters; "zombie institutions" are what sociologists call dead ideas from another age that still persist, often unquestioned, long after the life has gone out of them. Institutions become "zombified" when everyone *acts* as if they are still living—which invests them with undead power—even though they stopped being meaningful or useful long ago.[104] Zombified institutions are rigidly right-side-up—so one place to look for signs of divine action is when the tables of the temple are flipped for God's reconstruction.

Unofficial youth ministers—people driven by faith to help young people participate in God's reconstructing power but who do not work in formal youth ministry—often lead in this holy work. Noran Sanford, a United Methodist social worker and mental health therapist in Wagram, North Carolina, is one such title-less "youth minister" and zombie toppler. Sanford founded Growing Change[105] after attending the funeral of one of his middle school clients, who had been killed in a gang incident. Sanford said, "I had to be honest with myself that the system had not done everything it could do, that I had not done everything I could do."[106] So he began to pray—and suddenly took notice of the decaying Scotland Correctional Facility that he drove by

127

each day going to work. The Scotland Correctional Facility was *actually* a zombie institution—still standing, but decommissioned, no longer useful in today's society.

That is when it came to Sanford to "flip" a prison with teenagers.

Sanford invited a group of formerly incarcerated youth to walk through the prison property with him. When they finished, he handed them the keys. "What can we do with this?" he asked them.

What the youth imagined—and built—was an educational farm created and run by teenagers who have done time (today Growing Change also includes teenagers facing additional struggles). They keep bees, rotate a grazing herd of sheep for wool and meat, care for hens, compost waste, tend an organic garden, and more. When I met Sanford in 2017, he had just received plans from M.I.T. to realize another idea from his teenage board: turning the prison watch tower into a climbing wall.

Today, formerly incarcerated youth make up Sanford's board of directors. He appreciates the upside-down power dynamics in this arrangement ("I work for them," he told me). Growing Change does not have a single congregation or denomination in its partner list (though area churches widely support it). But there is no doubt: Sanford is knee-deep in upside-down youth ministry that was literally an answer to prayer.

Out Is In:
Homeboy Industries (Los Angeles, California)

What we are learning from ministries with the missing voices in Christian youth work—ministries that intentionally neighbor young people whom churches tend to overlook, intentionally or unintentionally, because they are in foster care, have disabilities, have intellectual or developmental disorders, or belong to a group (like LGBTQ+ young people) sometimes ostracized from Christian communities—is how much the church suffers when these young people are excluded from ministry.[107] A right-side-up church treats ministries with these youth as "niche": yes, these young people need particular kinds of attention, and yes, the church should "provide" something for them. As long as these niche ministries do not disrupt business as usual, they serve our right-side-up idea of church quite nicely.

The problem with this approach (besides being insufferably condescending) is that it distinguishes the server from the served, the "benevolent" church from the people "in need." Upside-down youth ministry, by contrast, makes no such distinctions; all of us are both server and served. All of us need Christ; all of us are called to offer Christ. Upside-down youth ministry erases the lines between who is "in" and who is "out" in the church. As Fr. Gregory Boyle puts it, we don't go to the margins to make a difference; we go to the margins to be made different.[108]

Almost thirty years ago, Boyle created a bakery to employ gang members no one else would hire. Homeboy Industries didn't stop there; it soon offered a café, a job training program, tattoo removal, and more. But here is the important point: Homeboy Industries is not really a collection of services for gang members. It is a haven where rival gang members, who might kill each other on the street, work side by side toward a common goal (and yes, they get job training along the way). A ministry that looks like a collection of "services" from the outside is really a crucible for holy friendship. What looks like "outreach" is—in no way—an attempt to "reach" gang members, or find a new market of youth ministry "customers." Everything about Homeboy Industries is aimed at relationships, because (to quote Boyle), this is how "God's dream comes true."[109]

Weak Is Strong:
Conetoe Family Life Center (Conetoe, NC)

This fall, my colleague Nate Stucky and I will once again take a class to rural Conetoe, North Carolina, to plant cabbages with the Rev. Richard Joyner. Joyner, named a "CNN Hero" in 2015, is the son of a sharecropper. Like many people in Conetoe, he hates farming. He became a pastor in part to avoid farming. He describes watching his father tend crops from dawn till dusk—only to receive almost nothing at the harvest. Generational anger seeped into Richard and his friends, who watched wealthy white landowners exploit their parents' sweaty, back-breaking work in ways that hearkened back to the way slave owners exploited the toil of their grandparents and great-grandparents.

After seeing harvest after harvest stolen from their families, Richard's generation grew up vowing to do *anything* with their lives except farm.

Richard remembers his parents protecting him from this anger, but says that he later learned that "internalized anger unexpressed can be as deadly to your health as anything else."[110] Poverty had created a food desert in Conetoe; obesity, asthma, and diabetes were rampant. One year the emergency squad made over 200 trips to Conetoe—for a population of 300 people. In one of his first years as a pastor, thirty people died, most of them young, mostly from preventable, diet-related diseases. Driving home after preaching the funeral of a thirty-year-old father, Richard was at the end of his rope. Each year when he tells our class about this moment, he remembers it with tears in his eyes: "I just couldn't look another child in the eye who had just lost her daddy and tell her everything would be all right…because that was a damn lie." Wracked with grief, he remembers pulling over to the side of the road and praying: "Lord, what do you want me to *do*?"

As the story goes, Richard heard a voice say, "Open your eyes. Look around you." When he did, he saw nothing but fields and land. "I said to God, 'Is there anybody else?! This is no time to be playin.'" But he knew he had his answer: He had to bring fresh food to Conetoe, and that meant farming.

He floated the idea at a congregational meeting. People were anything but receptive. This pastor was leading them back into slavery! They would be exploited for their labor and left with nothing. The meeting was heated.

Then a twelve-year-old girl got up to speak: "*Please*," she beseeched the congregation. "My daddy has died. My aunt has died. My grandmother died. Please help me. *I don't want to be left alone.*"

The adults begrudgingly told Richard that if he wanted to farm, he could, but don't expect any help from them. So he started a garden by the church—with a farm crew of children. What they lacked in strength they made up for in determination. They came after school and on weekends. Teenagers dug and ten-year-olds planted. All spring they tended beans and corn and tomatoes and squash. And when the crops came in, they proudly took their treasures home—and their families feasted on fresh vegetables for a season.

That year the number of emergency squad trips to Conetoe dropped to *three*. The local hospital was so shocked that they called Richard to see what was going on. It turned out that the pastor had started a garden with some kids.

Worship is still central to life in Conetoe; Richard preaches every Sunday. But his ministry, and his joy, comes from young people's leadership. Youth are the major stakeholders in the intergenerational Conetoe Family Life Center[111]—and they know their leadership has made a life-and-death difference to their community. Today, the Family Life Center farms produce enough fresh produce for Conetoe, and more to sell to the local hospital, increasing local health and income at the same time. It offers nutritional counseling, after school programs, summer camps, a farm stand, cooking classes, health and wellness programs, and a successful beekeeping business (the youth took a vote about the bees; Richard, who was opposed to it, got outvoted). The eleven-year-old with the idea became the youngest certified beekeeper in the state of North Carolina.

What the young people of Conetoe *don't* have—or need—is a "youth group."

ENDNOTES

1. Jeff Beer, "Six Experts Reveal the Post-Covid-19 Truth about the Advertising Business," *Fast Company*, May 27, 2020, https://www.fastcompany.com/90506224/six-experts-reveal-the-post-covid-truth-about-the-advertising-business (accessed January 20, 2021).

2. Emma Gonzalez, cited in "Florida Student Emma Gonzalez to Lawmakers and Gun Advocates: 'We Call B.S.'" [transcript], *CNN*, February 17, 2018, https://www.cnn.com/2018/02/17/us/florida-student-emma-gonzalez-speech/index.html (accessed July 27, 2020).

3. A second teenager active in the diocese, fourteen-year-old Cara Loughren, was also among the victims.

4. Julie Turkewitz, "Florida Students Began with Optimism. Then They Spoke to Lawmakers," *The New York Times*, February 21, 2018, https://www.nytimes.com/2018/02/21/us/tallahassee-parkland-students.html (accessed July 27, 2020).

5. See Jeremiah 18:1-6.

6. See Sid Schwarz, "The New Paradigm Spiritual Communities: Catalyzing the Field," concept paper, February 2016. Schwarz points out that young people creating new paradigm spiritual communities are not apostates; they are, in fact, young people who have been well-formed in their religious traditions but no longer see themselves in it. Schwarz writes about acculturated Judaism in Jonathan Woocher, ed., *Sacred Survival: The Civil Religion of American Jews* (Bloomington, IN: Indiana University Press, 1986).

7. I'm adapting this quote from Michael Goheen, writing about missiologist Leslie Newbigin, who put it this way: "The choice of the church in every age in every age will always be, Will our identity be shaped by Scripture or by our culture—by the Biblical story or by the cultural story?" The phrase is adapted here to avoid unintentional biblicism. Michael Goheen, *Church and Its Vocation* (Grand Rapids, MI: Baker Academic, 2018), 1.

8. Thanks to Pastor Harland Redmond, whose sermon on Philippians 3:7-14 articulated these ideas better than I could, and whose phrasing I have adapted here (Kingston United Methodist Church, Jan. 10, 2021).

9. Christian Smith and Melinda Denton, *Soul Searching: The Religious and Spiritual Lives of American Teenagers* (New York: Oxford University

Press, 2009), 162-163.

10. Smith and Denton note that moralistic therapeutic deism does not align with any of the world's great religions, and co-opts Christian, Jewish, and Islamic youth in similar ways, espousing similar superficial religious views. Smith and Denton, 163.

11. Smith and Denton, 171. Religious youth group participation, for example, has little impact on faith formation—though it offers important skills for navigating social institutions, a key feature of middle-class existence. For example, youth who attend religious youth groups feel more comfortable speaking with adults, have more adults they can turn to for support, adhere more closely to community moral norms, and find church less boring than other teenagers (for older youth ages 16-20, worship attendance affords the same benefits). See Patricia Snell, "What Difference Does Youth Group Make? A Longitudinal Analysis of Religious Youth Group Participation Outcomes," *The Journal for the Scientific Study of Religion* 48 (2009), especially pp. 577-584.

12. "The Odd History of Odd," *Merriam-Webster*, www.merriam-webster. com/words-at-play/the-odd-history-of-odd (accessed January 9, 2021).

13. Lesslie Newbigin, *The Gospel in a Pluralist Society* (Grand Rapids, MI: Eerdmans, 1989), 116.

14. See Kenda Creasy Dean, *Practicing Passion: Youth and the Quest for a Passionate Church* (Grand Rapids: Eerdmans, 2004), 17-19.

15. For a stark illustration of this risk, see Dietrich Brueggemann's 2014 movie *Stations of the Cross.*

16. Thanks to longtime youth minister Lars Rood for the phrase "sober virgins."

17. Smith and Denton, 171. This description fails to take into account changing patterns in the way faith is formed; cf. Abby Day, *Believing in Belonging: Belief and Social Identity in the Modern World* (London: Oxford University Press), 2013.

18. Smith and Denton, 171.

19. "The State of Religion and Young People 2020" (Bloomington, MN: Springtide Research Institute, 2020), 24.

20. In 2020, the Pew Research Center puts the number of youth for whom religion is very important at 24%. "Religious Beliefs among American Adolescents," *Pew Research Center*, September 10, 2020, https://www. pewforum.org/2020/09/10/religious-beliefs-among-american-adoles-cents/ (accessed January 22, 2021).

21. In particular, studies that measure religious disaffiliation could include some young people who consider themselves both religiously unaffiliated and religiously devoted. We're not comparing apples and oranges here, but we may be comparing different kinds of apples.

22. "State of Religion and Young People 2020," 38ff.

23. Dietrich Bonhoeffer, *The Cost of Discipleship* (New York: Touchstone, 1995), 89.

24. Donald Kraybill, *The Upside-Down Kingdom* (Harrisonburg, VA: Herald Press, 2011), 71-72. See Matthew 4 and Luke 4.

25. Howard Thurman, *Jesus and the Disinherited* (Boston: Beacon Press, 1996), 7. For the importance of Thurman for youth ministry, see Stephen Cady, "Creative Encounters: Toward a Theology of Magnitude for Worship with United Methodist Youth," unpublished dissertation (Princeton Theological Seminary), 2014.

26. Katharine Q. Seelye, "John Lewis, Towering Figure of Civil Rights Era, Dies at 80," *The New York Times,* July 17, 2020, https://www.nytimes.com/2020/07/17/us/john-lewis-dead.html (accessed January 17, 2020).

27. John Lewis, extended interview, *Religion and Ethics Newsweekly,* January 16, 2004, https://www.pbs.org/wnet/religionandethics/2004/01/16/january-16-2004-john-lewis-extended-interview/2897/ (accessed January 23, 2021).

28. Kraybill, 255.

28a. Kraybill.

29. Pinetops Foundation, *The Great Opportunity*, https://www.greatopportunity.org.

30. Wallace Witkowski, "Video games are a bigger industry than movies and North American sports combined, thanks to the pandemic," *Market Watch,* December 22, 2020, https://www.marketwatch.com/story/videogames-are-a-bigger-industry-than-sports-and-movies-combined-thanks-to-the-pandemic-11608654990.

31. The whole curriculum is free through the Urban Youth Workers Institute: https://uywi.uscreen.io/programs/developing-digital-disciples.

32. Career Wise Colorado, "Infographic: Mentorship Opportunities Gen Z," https://www.careerwisecolorado.org/en/infographic-mentorship-empowers-gen-z-employees/.

33. "Mentorship Opportunities Gen Z."

34. For a deeper dive into Rick's approach, see *Jesus Centered Youth Ministry*

(Loveland, CO: Group Publishing, 2014).

35. Rick describes this process in more detail in his article, "Reboot" in the 2019 special edition of *GROUP* Magazine.

36. Rick Lawrence, "Killing the Cockroach" *YouthMinistry.com*, https://youthministry.com/killing-the-cockroach/ (accessed January 26, 2021).

37. By way of comparison, when I was in seminary in the mid-1980s, there was a single (1) course call "Christian Education of Youth." Today that institution has a highly acclaimed Institute for Youth Ministry and a rippling variety of classes offered in the field.

38. This pattern has been much less prevalent in churches of color, where creative models of youth ministry emerged, often in response to financial realities. But even in churches of color that had resources, most were slow to adopt the model of the full-time youth worker.

39. Dan McPherson, "Dying Trends in Youth Ministry," *YS Blog,* July 9, 2019, https://blog.youthspecialties.com/5-dying-trends-in-youth-ministry/.

40. Summy Lau, "How Different Generations Are Supporting Charity in 2019: Infographic," *Winspire News,* https://blog.winspireme.com/generational-giving-infographic-2019 (accessed January 26, 2021).

41. Sara Dehoff, "A Look At Generational Differences in Giving," *Greater Giving,* August 29, 2019, https://blog.greatergiving.com/a-look-at-generational-differences-in-giving/.

42. Barna Group, "The Priorities, Challenges, and Trends in Ministry," *Barna,* April 6, 2016, https://www.barna.com/research/the-priorities-challenges-and-trends-in-youth-ministry/.

43. Wendy McCormick, "Thriving Youth Ministry in Small Churches," *Center for Congregations,* https://centerforcongregations.org/blog/thriving-youth-ministry-small-churches) (accessed January 26, 2021).

44. Sam Rainer, "What Two Simple Statistics Reveal about the American Church," *Sam Rainer,* January 21, 2018, https://samrainer.com/2018/01/what-two-simple-statistics-reveal-about-the-american-church/. This same pattern is echoed in by the Hartford Institute for Religion Research: http://hirr.hartsem.edu/research/fastfacts/fast_facts.html#size-cong.

45. Christians Struggled with Relational Health Prior to the Crisis—So What Has Changed?" *Barna,* September 23, 2020, https://www.barna.com/research/christians-relational-health/.

46. Thom S. Rainer, "Six Reasons Your Youth Pastor Is About To Quit," *Church Answers*, August 31, 2020, https://churchanswers.com/blog/six-reasons-your-pastor-is-about-to-quit/.

47. David Kinnaman, "New Trends: 4 Ways the Pandemic Is Negatively Impacting People," *Carey Nieuwhof*, https://careynieuwhof.com/new-trends-4-ways-the-pandemic-is-negatively-impacting-people/).

48. Ministry Incubators: https://ministryincubators.com/.

49. Try Pie: https://www.trypie.org/.

50. Shared in an email from Sarah to Mark, December 2020.

51. MowTown Teen Lawn Care: https://www.facebook.com/Mowtown-Teen-Lawn-Care-362123533987508/.

52. "MowTown Teen Lawn Care is a social enterprise offering a new model for youth ministry," *Faith & Leadership*, https://faithandleadership.com/mowtown-teen-lawn-care-social-enterprise-offering-new-model-youth-ministry.

53. The Columbia Future Forge: www.thecolumbiafutureforge.com.

54. Matt Overton, *Mentorship and Marketplace: A New Direction for Youth Ministry* (San Diego: The Youth Cartel, 2019).

55. Go Fish!: https://www.gofishppc.org/.

56. Go Fish!

57. "Amateur," *Wordnik*, https://www.wordnik.com/words/amateur.

58. The young people I have sent have loved all of the Youth Theology Network (https://fteleaders.org/networks/ytn) experiences funded by the Lilly Endowment and coordinated by the Fund for Theological Education.

59. The Changemaker Initiative: https://thechangemakerinitiative.org/.

60. Ministry Incubators Hatchathons: https://ministryincubators.com/offerings/hatchathons/.

61. William H. Frey, "What the 2020 Census Will Reveal About America," January 11, 2021, https://www.brookings.edu/research/what-the-2020-census-will-reveal-about-america-stagnating-growth-an-aging-population-and-youthful-diversity/ (accessed January 15, 2021).

62. William H. Frey, "Diversity Explosion," *Brookings,* July 24, 2018, https://www.brookings.edu/book/diversity-explosion-2/ (accessed December 28, 2020).

63. Reggie Joiner, *The Orange Strategy* (Cumming, GA: The reThink Group,

Inc., 2016), 19.

64. "Family," *Merriam-Webster*, https://www.merriam-webster.com/dictionary/family.

65. Dick Iverson et al., *Restoring the Family: Principles of Family Life* (Portland, OR: Bible Temple Publications, 1979).

66. "Family," *Open Education Sociological Dictionary*, https://sociologydictionary.org/family/.

67. "Family," *Love to Know*, https://family.lovetoknow.com/definition-family.

68. Pew Research Center, "Parenting in America," December 17, 2015, https://www.pewsocialtrends.org/2015/12/17/1-the-american-family-today/ (accessed January 28, 2021).

69. US Census was the first decennial census to collect this data beginning in 2000 and reports a steady rate of 15% in 2009, and 16% in 2015: United States Census Bureau, National Stepfamily Day: September 16, 2020," *United States Census Bureau* (September 16, 2020), https://www.census.gov/newsroom/stories/stepfamily-day.html (accessed January 17, 2021).

70. LeAlan Jones and Lloyd Newman, *Our America: Life and Death on the South Side of Chicago* (New York: Pocket Books, 1997).

71. Ana Patricia Muñoz, Marlene Kim, Mariko Chang, Regine O. Jackson, Darrick Hamilton, and William A. Darity Jr., "The Color of Wealth in Boston," March 25, 2015, https://www.bostonfed.org/publications/one-time-pubs/color-of-wealth.aspx.

72. Muñoz et al., "The Color of Wealth in Boston."

73. Jawanza Kunjufu, *Motivating and Preparing Black Youth for Success* (Chicago: African American Images, 1986), 16.

74. Muñoz et al., "The Color of Wealth in Boston." Chart reprinted thanks to permission from the Federal Reserve Bank of Boston.

75. Ortiz Conn, *Urban Ministry: The Kingdom, the City and the People of God* (Downers Grove, IL: IVP Academic, 2001), 129.

76. Adam McCann, "Most & Least Ethnically Diverse Cities in the U.S.," *Wallet Hub* (February 11, 2020), https://wallethub.com/edu/cities-with-the-most-and-least-ethno-racial-and-linguistic-diversity/10264 (accessed December 28, 2020).

77. David Livermore, *The Cultural Intelligence Difference: Master the One Skill You Can't Do Without in Today's Global Economy* (New York: American Management Association, 2011), 5.

78. Eugene C. Roehlkepartain, *Building Assets in Congregations: A Practical Guide for Helping Youth Grow Up Healthy* (Minneapolis, MN: Search Institute, 1998), 31.

79. Markham Heid, "Depression and Suicide Rates Are Rising Sharply in Young Americans, New Report Says. This May Be One Reason Why," *Time*, March 14, 2019, https://time.com/5550803/depression-suicide-rates-youth/. Based on a study published in the *Journal of Abnormal Psychology*.

80. Edwin H. Friedman, *Generation to Generation: Family Process in Church and Synagogue* (New York: The Guilford Press, 2011), ix.

81. Andrew Root, *The End of Youth Ministry?* (Grand Rapids, MI: Baker Academic, 2020), xii.

82. Chris Shirley, *Family Ministry and the Church: A Leader's Guide for Ministry* (Nashville, TN: Randall House Publications, 2018), 12.

83. Shirley, *Family Ministry and the Church,* 17.

84. Kara Powell, "Can Social Distancing Reinvent Youth Ministry?" *Christianity Today*, April 15, 2020), https://www.christianitytoday.com/pastors/2020/april-web-exclusives/coronavirus-social-distancing-reinvent-youth-ministry.html.

85. Steven M. Constantino, *Engage Every Family: Five Simple Principles* (Thousand Oaks, CA: Corwin, 2016).

86. Think Orange: thinkorange.com.

87. Reggie Joiner, Kristen Ivy and Virginia Ward, *It's Personal: Five Questions You Should Answer to Give Every Kid Hope* (Cumming, GA: The reThink Group, Inc, 2019), 10.

88. Reggie Joiner, *Orange Essentials* (Cummin, GA: The reThink Group, Inc., 2013), 23.

89. Dr. Sarah Williams, "A Theology for the Rebellion," *Youthscape*, St. Mellitus Annual Lecture 2020, youthscape.co.uk/lecture.

90. Naomi Thompson, *Young People and Church Since 1900: Engagement and Exclusion (AHRC/ESRC Religion and Society Series)* (London: Routledge, 2017).

91. Quoted in Milton Rokeach, *The Open and Closed Mind: Investigations into the Nature of Belief Systems and Personality Systems* (Eastford, CT: Martino Fine Books, 2015).

92. Jean M. Twenge, *iGen: Why Today's Super-Connected Kids Are Growing Up Less Rebellious, More Tolerant, Less Happy—and Completely Unpre-*

pared for Adulthood—and What That Means for the Rest of Us (New York: Atria Books, 2017).

93. Dr. Lucie Shuker, "Faith in Young People: Challenges and opportunities for youth ministry in the Diocese of St. Albans," unpublished research, 2021.

94. John Glenn, "Interview for Objects of Wonder exhibition," The Ohio State University, 2008. https://www.youtube.com/watch?v=iltObvPpf-Do&feature=emb_logo (accessed February 2021).

95. Albert Einstein, statement to William Miller, as quoted in *Life* magazine, (May 2, 1955).

96. Willian Inge, *Diary of a Dean* (London: Hutchinson, 1949).

97. "Burning Down the House: How the church could lose young people over climate inaction," Co-published by *Tearfund* and the *Youthscape Centre for Research* (February 2021), https://weare.tearfund.org/wp-content/uploads/2021/02/Burning-Down-The-House-Youthscape-and-Tearfund.pdf.

98. Charles Taylor, *A Secular Age* (Cambridge, MA: Belknap Press, 2007).

99. Taylor, *A Secular Age*.

100. "Losing Heart," *The Youthscape Centre for Research* (2015), https://www.youthscape.co.uk/research/losing-heart.

101. 2 Corinthians 4:8.

102. L. Morris, "Faith" in Marshall et al., *New Bible Dictionary* (Downers Grove, IL: InterVarsity Press, 1996), 360.

103. Mark Sayers, *Reappearing Church: The Hope for Renewal in the Rise of Our Post-Christian Culture* (Chicago: Moody Publishers, 2019), 9.

104. Cf. Beck, U. & Beck-Gersheim, E. "Zombie Categories: Interview with Ulrich Beck," in P. Camiller (trans.), *Individualization: Institutionalized Individualism and its Social and Political Consequences* 13 (London: Sage, 2002), pp. 202–213; also Whelan, A., Walker, R. & Moore, C., eds., *Zombies in the Academy: Living Death in Higher Education* (Chicago, IL: The University of Chicago Press), 2013.

105. http://www.growingchange.org/.

106. Christina Cook, "Youth Are Flipping an Abandoned North Carolina Prison into a Sustainable Farm," *Civil Eats*, June 15, 2020, https://civileats.com/2020/06/15/youth-are-flipping-an-abandoned-north-carolina-prison-into-a-sustainable-farm/ (accessed January 22, 2021).

107. The Missing Voices Project at Flagler College empowers congregations to address young people often invisible to or unwelcome in churches; see https://missingvoices.flagler.edu/; also see Benjamin Connor, *Amplifying Our Witness: Giving Voice to Adolescents with Developmental Disabilities* (Grand Rapids, MI: Eerdmans, 2012).

108. For more on this theme, listen to Fr. Gregory Boyle, "Kinship: What Leaning from the Margins Looks Like," *The Missing Voices Podcast* 16, May 27, 2020, https://missingvoicesproject.podbean.com/e/16-gregory-boyle%e2%80%a6-kinship-what-learning-from-the-margins-looks-like/ (accessed January 19, 2021).

109. Gregory Boyle, *Barking to the Choir: The Power of Radical Kinship* (New York: Simon and Schuster, 2017), 17.

110. Laura Pellicer and Frank Stasio, "The Reluctant Farmer: Meet Richard Joyner," *WUNC 91.5/North Carolina Public Radio*, August 14, 2017, https://www.wunc.org/post/reluctant-farmer-meet-reverend-richard-joyner (accessed January 19, 2021).

111. conetoelife.org.

BIOS

Mark Oestreicher is a partner in The Youth Cartel, which provides resources, training, and coaching for church youth workers, and is the author of many books for youth workers, parents, and teenagers. Twitter: @ markosbeard.

Chris Curtis works with young people in the UK. He's part of Youthscape, a ministry focused on innovation in church youth ministry. In his spare time he's a bit of a Mac nerd and a member of The Magic Circle.

Kenda Creasy Dean is an ordained United Methodist pastor and the Mary D. Synnott Professor of Youth, Church, and Culture at Princeton Theological Seminary, where she works closely with the Institute for Youth Ministry and the Farminary. In 2013 she founded Ministry Incubators with fellow youth pastor and serial entrepreneur Mark DeVries, to support Christian leaders in faith-based social innovation. Her most recent books include *Knee-Deep in Flotsam: Why Churches Innovate and How to Start,* and *Delighted: What Teenagers Are Teaching the Church about Joy.* She and her husband, Kevin, live in Princeton, New Jersey, and are the parents of two hilarious grown children.

Mark DeVries is the founder and president of Ministry Architects and the co-founder of Ministry Incubators. From 1986 through 2014 he served as the Associate Pastor for Youth and Their Families at First Presbyterian Church in Nashville, Tennessee. Mark is the author of books including *Sustainable Youth Ministry* and *Family-Based Youth Ministry*. He and his wife, Susan, make their home in Nashville, and have three grown children and four grandchildren.

Tommy Nixon is a founder and former Executive Director of Solidarity, a nonprofit organization that strengthens urban communities. Tommy is currently the Chief Executive Officer for Urban Youth Workers Institute, leading the organization to empower urban youth workers to become the leaders and role models urban youth need to live lives transformed by the gospel of Jesus Christ. Tommy lives in Anaheim, CA, has been married to Rachael since 2003, and has four amazing daughters and one son.

Virginia Ward is the Dean of the Boston Campus and Executive Director of the Northeast Region of Gordon-Conwell Theological Seminary, where she teaches classes in youth ministry and leadership. She also serves as an Associate Pastor at the Abundant Life Church in Cambridge, Massachusetts, where her husband, Bishop Lawrence Ward, is the lead pastor. Together they formed a consulting company, Wards of Wisdom, to support urban ministries seeking change. Virginia and her husband reside in Boston and have two adult sons.

Made in the USA
Columbia, SC
19 July 2021